This book
belongs to

....

Amazing History facts

Amazing
History
facts

Written by
Richard Tames, Rupert Matthews,
Margarette Lincoln, and Fiona Corbridge

Edited by
Paul Harrison, Nicola Wright, Dee Turner, and Fiona Mitchell

zigzag

CONTENTS

ANCIENT TIMES 6

WARRIORS 34

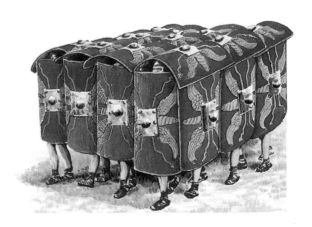

Under Babylonian law, a son who hit his father had his hands chopped off.

The oldest known civilizations began in the area we now call the Middle East. Some cities, such as Damascus and Jericho, are at least 5,000 years old.

Q How big were the earliest cities?

A The earliest cities were nowhere near as large as modern cities. Çatal Hüyük, in what is now Turkey, was built about 9,000 years ago and had a population of only 5,000. The houses were made of mud bricks and were built up against each other, so there were no streets. People got in and out of their houses through holes in the roof using ladders.

Q What did the Sumerians invent?

A The Sumerians knew how to weave cloth, make things out of metal and make pots on a wheel. But the most important progress they made was in writing, mathematics and astronomy. Their discoveries in these areas enabled them to keep records of taxes and agreements, write down laws and work out a calendar.

Q Where was Mesopotamia?

A Mesopotamia means "the land between the rivers." The area was in what is now Iraq. The rivers were the Tigris and the Euphrates, and the first city dwellers there were known as Sumerians. By 3000 B.C. there were powerful city states, such as Ur and Uruk, which traded with and fought against each other. The cities had populations of up to 50,000 people and were often built around mud-brick temples called ziggurats.

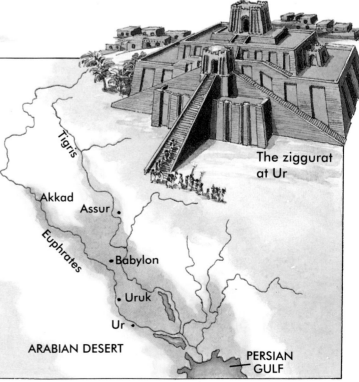

The ziggurat at Ur

Tigris

Akkad

Assur

Euphrates

Babylon

Uruk

Ur

ARABIAN DESERT

PERSIAN GULF

The oldest known set of false teeth belonged to a Phoenician man of 1000 B.C. He had four of someone else's teeth tied to his own with gold wire.

Sargon of Akkad

Q What was their writing like?

A The first writing was pictographic. This means that instead of using letters and words, the Sumerians drew pictures. Later, these pictures came to represent sounds rather than actual objects. Sumerian writing is called "cuneiform," which means "wedge-shaped," because they used a sharp wedge to make marks in the clay tablets on which they wrote.

Q Which were the most powerful city states?

A Sargon of Akkad (2370 B.C.) was the first great conqueror that we know about. The Hittites created an empire based around Anatolia between 1800 B.C. and 1200 B.C. The Assyrians were a war-like people from the city state of Assur. They built a huge empire stretching from the Persian Gulf to Egypt, between 800 B.C. and 650 B.C.

Cuneiform writing

Q Where did civilization begin in in the Mediterranean?

A The Minoan people began to build palaces on the island of Crete around 2200 B.C. The Palace of Knossos could hold up to 80,000 people. Around 1400 B.C. the Minoans were conquered by the Mycenaeans from mainland Greece.

7

Chess was invented in ancient India as a war game.

The Indus Valley stretches from Tibet, through Pakistan, to the Indian Ocean. The River Indus flows through this valley. Many ancient towns have been discovered there.

Q What was life like in the Indus Valley?

A Two major cities, called Mohenjo Daro and Harappa, have been found in this area, along with the sites of over one hundred other towns. From these ruins scientists have been able to discover many things about this ancient civilization. However, archaeologists have not been able to read the type of writing used by the Indus people at this time, so we still know very little about the way they lived.

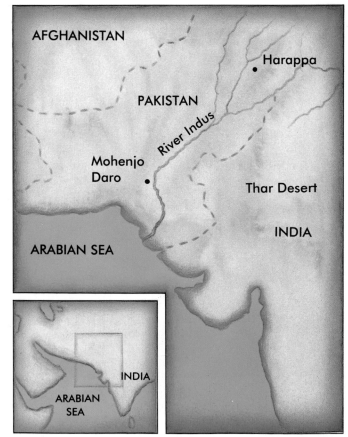

Q How long ago did these cities exist?

A They were probably built around 2500 B.C. and later abandoned around 1500 B.C. Each one was nearly 3 miles in circumference. No one is quite sure why these cities were abandoned, but the most likely explanation is that the Indus River changed course, moving away from the cities.

Q Why were cities built in this area?

A The people of the Indus Valley relied on the annual flooding of the river to provide the mineral-rich silt that made the farmland fertile. Owing to this, all the major towns and cities were built close to the river.

Merchants in Mohenjo Daro used to stamp their goods with seals. Nobody is sure if different merchants used different pictures on their seals, but there have been many different sorts found.

Q Was life in Mohenjo Daro well organized?

A The city was laid out on a rigid street plan and had the world's first known sewer system with drains and manholes. There were wide streets and large granaries for storing food in case the harvest failed. Houses were made out of bricks that were the same size, rather than oddly-shaped pieces of stone. Each house also had its own bathroom and toilet.

Q How did people dress?

A The Indus Valley people were the first in the world to grow cotton and make it into cloth. They also used copper to make jewelery. Men made razors out of copper.

Q What sort of transport did people use?

A Two-wheeled ox carts carried heavy loads over land, and boats were used to transport things up and down the river. Camels and pack horses were used to carry merchants' goods over long distances.

Q What did people do in their spare time?

A They kept pets such as dogs, cats, monkeys, caged birds and insects. Children played with whistles and toys, like pottery monkeys, which danced on pieces of string. Adults played dice games.

What is a dynasty?

荷葉飯

China has the oldest continuous civilization in the world. The country was ruled by different royal families known as dynasties. Little is known about the earliest part of Chinese history.

Q Where did civilization begin in China?

A The first powerful kingdom we know about was based near the fertile Yellow River around 1500 B.C. and was ruled by the Shang Dynasty. In 1027 B.C. the Shang were driven out by the Zhou, who ruled for 800 years.

Q What is the Great Wall of China?

A The Great Wall is the longest wall in the world. It is 2,150 miles long, stretching from the coast to the Gobi Desert. It was meant to keep out invaders from the north, but didn't always do so. The wall was built between 221 B.C. and 206 B.C., and strengthened by later emperors. Most of the present wall was rebuilt during the Ming Period (1368-1644).

Q Who was the first Emperor of the whole of China?

A In 221 B.C. the cruel and ruthless Qin ruler, Cheng, began to call himself Emperor of China. The Qin had overthrown the Zhou in 225 B.C. and ruled the biggest empire seen in history up to that time. Cheng also built the Great Wall of China.

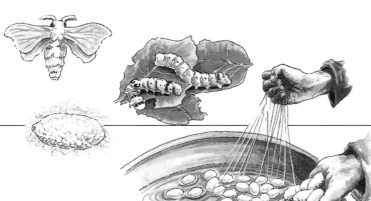

Smoke signals and kites were used to send messages along the Great Wall.

Q Why was silk important?

A Silk was China's main export, sent right across Asia, and even as far as Rome, along trading routes that became known as the "Silk Route." The silk came from the cocoons of silkworms and made a light, soft, strong thread. The Chinese learned how to rear silkworms, feeding them on mulberry leaves. They kept the secret of how to make silk to themselves until 550 A.D., when two Persian monks smuggled silkworms out of China in a hollow cane.

Q What did the Chinese invent?

A The Chinese discovered many different things, including how to make paper and porcelain, a kind of fine pottery. They also discovered that the resin of the lacquer tree could be used to coat wooden bowls so they could hold hot foods and liquids, such as soup. Wheelbarrows were in use a thousand years before they became common in Europe.

Q Who was Confucius ?

A Confucius was a scholar whose ideas about government were influential in China, as well as in other countries. He thought that peace and order were the greatest blessings a country could have. He believed that a ruler should be just and kind and his subjects should be loyal and obedient. Confucius also taught the importance of good manners and self-control.

Q What advances did the Chinese make in science?

A Wang Chong, who lived in the first century A.D., showed that eclipses and the movements of the stars and the moon could be predicted. Zhang Heng made the world's first seismograph, used to detect and record earthquakes. The Chinese also invented a kind of medicine, called acupuncture, which cures people by sticking needles in them.

Pictured is a seismograph. Balls dropped into the frogs' mouths when an earthquake occurred. The more balls that fell, the stronger the earthquake.

The Olmecs carved large stone heads which were up to 8.8 feet high.

People migrated from Asia to the American mainland about 30,000 years ago. Sea levels were lower then, and North America was joined to Russia by a land bridge. The first advanced civilizations grew up in Central America.

Q Which were the first important civilizations that we know of?

A The Olmecs lived along the eastern coast of what is now Mexico. Their civilization flourished between 1150 B.C. and 800 B.C. Their sculptures and pottery influenced later cultures. The Maya, from what is now Guatemala, were also important. They flourished between 300 B.C. and 900 A.D.

Q How advanced were they?

A The people of Central America knew about farming, pottery and writing and how to make things out of gold, copper and jade. They also made paper from the bark of wild fig trees. However, they had no knowledge of such things as iron, glass, coins, or the plough.

Q What did the people of Central America eat?

A The basic diet was made up of maize, beans, tomatoes, chili peppers and turkeys. People also reared dogs and guinea pigs to eat.

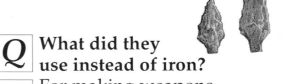

Q What did they use instead of iron?

A For making weapons and cutting tools they used obsidian, a kind of volcanic glass. When it is polished, obsidian has a very sharp edge, though it does break easily.

The Mayas used melted rubber to make waterproof clothing.

Chocolate was first brought to Europe from Central America, where it was made with chilli peppers.

Q Did they know about the wheel?

A They knew about the wheel but only used it on toys and not for transport. This was probably because they had no animal strong enough to pull a cart.

Q What was their religion like?

A They worshipped gods who represented the Sun, Moon, rain and maize. Human sacrifice was common and caused many wars as city states wanted to capture prisoners to sacrifice.

Q Can any of the cities still be seen?

A About forty cities have been discovered so far. The most important buildings were stepped pyramids, used for religious ceremonies. Teotihuacan (which means "Where Men become Gods"), near modern Mexico City, had a population of 200,000 and covered 7.7 sq. mi. The main street was 1.2 mi. long and 130 ft. wide, with over a hundred temples along its sides. The largest building, the Pyramid of the Sun, was over 230 feet high.

Q Did they play games?

A We know that they played a game which involved hitting a hard rubber ball at stone markers along the sides of a walled court. Heads, elbows, knees and shoulders could be used to hit the ball, but you could not use hands or feet. During festivals games were played in honor of the gods, and the loser became a human sacrifice.

Were there cities in Africa?

The oldest human remains in the world have been found in Tanzania.

Ancient Africa's greatest civilization developed in Egypt. But there were other important states along its northern coast and in what are now the present-day countries of Sudan and Ethiopia.

Q Did people ever live in the Sahara?

A The Sahara has not always been a desert, and people used to live there until 2000 B.C. Historians know they herded cattle, made pottery, and used four-wheeled vehicles, either as war chariots or as carts for transport.

Q What happened after the Sahara had become a desert?

A The Sahara started to dry up around 10,000 B.C. Some people still managed to live in oases where there was enough water for date palms and their livestock. By using camels, which could go without water for days, traders were able to cross 186 miles of desert in a week. They bought salt and cloth from the north in exchange for slaves, gold and leather from the south.

Q What was Carthage?

A Carthage was originally a colony, founded near present-day Tunis, by the Phoenicians. They were a trading people who lived in what is now Lebanon. In their language it was called Kart-Hadasht, which means "New Town." Carthage grew rich and powerful through trade and its silver mines.

Q What happened to Carthage?

A The Romans feared the growing power of Carthage, and fought three great wars over a hundred years. The Romans were finally victorious in 146 B.C. They totally destroyed Carthage and ploughed up the land where it had once stood.

Q Which was the first great empire of eastern Africa?

A The kingdom of Kush, probably founded by people from Egypt, rose on the banks of the Nile River. The kings of Kush were buried in pyramids, like Egyptian pharaohs. The first capital of Kush was founded at Napata, on a bend of the Nile. The kingdom grew rich on the gold it traded with Egypt. After Napata was attacked, the capital was moved to Meroe on the other bank of the Nile.

Q What happened to Kush?

A Kush was a great kingdom for a thousand years. There is evidence of iron production and a high level of trading along the Nile. There were also great palaces and a temple to the Egyptian god, Amon. However, the Kush were overthrown by their neighbor, Aksum, around 300 A.D.

Q How did the kingdom of Aksum grow?

A Aksum was probably founded by a mixture of African and southern Arabian peoples. The capital, also called Aksum, was in the highlands, and there was an important port, called Adulis, which was a major trading point. From 300 B.C. to A.D. 600. Aksum grew rich on the ivory trade.

Q What can be seen of Aksum today?

A Aksum lies in what is now Ethiopia. The ruins of Aksum include a palace with twenty-seven carved thrones. There are also 126 granite columns, some over 98 feet high. Other columns are carved with pictures of multistory houses.

Q Did the Ancient Africans use iron?

A People living around Nok in Nigeria were making iron tools and weapons by about 5000 B.C. By A.D. 400 the use of iron had spread all the way down to southern Africa.

When was Egypt formed?

Pharaoh Ramesses II reigned for sixty-seven years and had over one hundred children.

Lower Egypt, the area around the Nile delta, and Upper Egypt were united under one ruler around 3100 B.C. The Egyptian civilization lasted until 30 B.C., when Egypt became part of the Roman Empire.

Q Why was the ruler called pharaoh?

A The Egyptians thought that their ruler was descended from the Sun god and it would not be respectful for an ordinary person to use his name. They referred to him as pharaoh, or "per a' o" as the Egyptians called him, which means "The Great House."

Q What did the Egyptians call their country?

A The Egyptians called their country "Kmt," which means "The Black Land." This refers to the rich soil along the riverbanks. The desert on either side of the Nile which protected Egypt from invasion by enemies and provided gold and gem stones was called "Dsrt," which means "The Red Land."

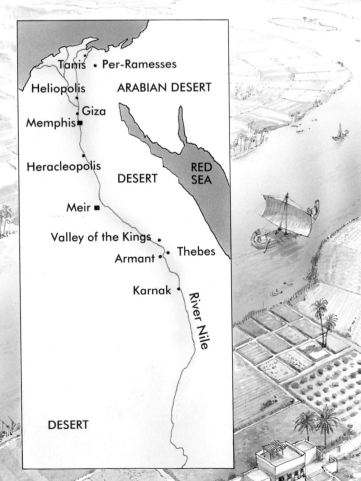

Tanis • Per-Ramesses
Heliopolis
ARABIAN DESERT
Giza
Memphis
Heracleopolis
DESERT
RED SEA
Meir
Valley of the Kings
Armant • Thebes
Karnak
River Nile
DESERT

Q Where was the capital?

A The site of the capital changed at different times. The first was at Memphis, midway between Upper and Lower Egypt. During the Middle Kingdom the capital city was further south at Itj-towy. The New Kingdom pharaohs made Thebes the capital and a great religious center. The later capitals of Per-Ramesses and Tanis were in the Nile delta.

The Egyptians were the first people to have bathrooms.

The Egyptians made sticky bandages out of linen coated with honey.

Q When was Egyptian civilization at its height?

A Egypt was at its greatest during periods which historians call the Old Kingdom (2575-2134 B.C.), the Middle Kingdom (2040-1640 B.C.) and the New Kingdom (1552-1070 B.C.). Between these times the country was torn by civil war and after the New Kingdom it was invaded by Assyrians, Persians and Greeks.

Q Did they conquer other kingdoms?

A During the New Kingdom the pharoahs built up a powerful army of infantry and charioteers. They built an empire which stretched from Syria in the north to Sudan in the south.

Q Was the River Nile important?

A Not only did the River Nile give the Egyptians fish and duck to eat, its annual flooding left a rich layer of silt on its banks which made the soil fertile again. Papyrus reeds grew in the river. These could be made into baskets, mats, brushes and paper. The river also made trade possible as it could be used to transport goods, even heavy objects such as stone. Around ninety percent of Egyptians lived within 6 mi. of the Nile or its marshy delta.

Q Did Egypt trade with other countries?

A Egypt traded gold in return for cedar wood from Lebanon, and oil, wine and silver from lands further afield. Ebony, ivory and incense came from countries south of Egypt.

What was life like in Egypt?

Egyptian mothers gave their children beer to take to school for their lunch.

Historians have a good idea what life was like in Egypt thanks to documents written on papyrus, inscriptions on stone and wall paintings and objects found in tombs.

Q What did people wear?

A Due to the hot climate, people needed only light clothes, usually made of linen. Often clothes were not worn indoors. Slaves, laborers and children usually went naked. However, people cared very much about their appearance and keeping clean. Both men and women wore eye makeup, jewelery and perfume.

Q What were their houses like?

A Homes, and even royal palaces, were made from sun-dried mud bricks. Stone was only used for tombs and temples. The hot weather and bright light meant that windows were small and placed high in the wall. Doors and windows often had screens made of matting to keep out flies and dust. In the hottest weather people slept on the flat roof.

Q How did they amuse themselves?

A Wall paintings show women dancing and having picnics, and men wrestling and hunting duck, antelopes and hares. Board games were popular with adults as well as children, and many families kept pets.

Q Did people eat well?

A The Nile provided fish, eels, ducks and geese. Fruit, vegetables and pork were also important parts of the daily diet. The Egyptians introduced the watermelon from southern Africa and the fig from Turkey. They also knew how to make wine, beer and cheese. Wheat was used to make pastry and biscuits, often flavored with honey and herbs, and forty different kinds of bread.

Egyptian gods. From left to right: Hathor, Toth, Anubis, Osiris and Isis.

Q Was religion important?

A The fact that the Egyptians built so many huge temples shows that religion was very important to them. They worshipped many different gods and believed that there was life after death. This belief led them to preserve the bodies of the dead as mummies, and to bury them with food, tools and weapons for the afterlife. Priests were very powerful. Ordinary people believed they could tell the future from dreams and the stars, and even protect them from evil with charms and spells.

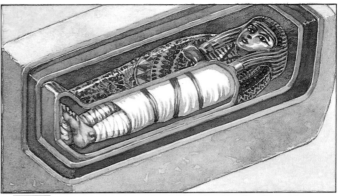

Q How were bodies made into mummies?

A The body was cut open and the heart, lungs and other organs were taken out and kept separately in a set of jars. The brain was pulled out through the nose with a hook, bit by bit, and thrown away. The body was then filled with natron, a natural salt which dried it out and stopped it from rotting. It was then stuffed with cloths and rolled in bandages before being buried inside two or three coffins. The whole business took about seventy days.

Q What work did people do?

A Most people were farmers. When there was no work in the fields they had time to help with the building of temples or pyramids. This was also a way of paying taxes. Skilled craftsmen were well paid, but they were paid in food, linen, firewood or salt, rather than money. Most women looked after their families, but they could also be weavers, dancers, nannies, priestesses, or makers of perfume and makeup.

Q When did people work?

A People worked for eight days at a time and then had two days rest. There were also 65 holy days set aside for ceremonies and festivals. People also took time off for funerals and birthdays. Most work was done in two shifts during the cooler times of the day - morning and evening. People took a nap during the heat of midday.

The pyramids at Giza once had smooth sides but the outer stones have been removed, leaving the step shape we see today.

Egypt's dry desert air has preserved many of its ancient treasures. Modern Egypt's tourist industry is based on taking visitors to famous sites and museums.

Q **Why were the pyramids built?**

A Pyramids were built to guard the bodies of dead pharaohs and their treasures. The first pyramids were built before the Old Kingdom and had sides rising in steps. The pyramids at Giza were built during the Old Kingdom, and are the only one of the Seven Wonders of the Ancient World which can be seen today.

Q **Which was the biggest pyramid?**

A The pyramid built for Khufu is 755.9 ft. along each side and was originally 469 ft. high. Its four sides face exactly north, south, east and west. Around 2,300,000 blocks of stone were needed to build it, each one averaging over two tons and the largest weighing 17 tons. It took 100,000 men over twenty years to build it.

Q **Who was Tutankhamun?**

A Tutankhamun became pharaoh when he was nine years old and died at the age of nineteen in 1352 B.C. His tomb was discovered in 1922. Unlike almost all the other royal tombs it had not been robbed and was filled with wonderful treasures.

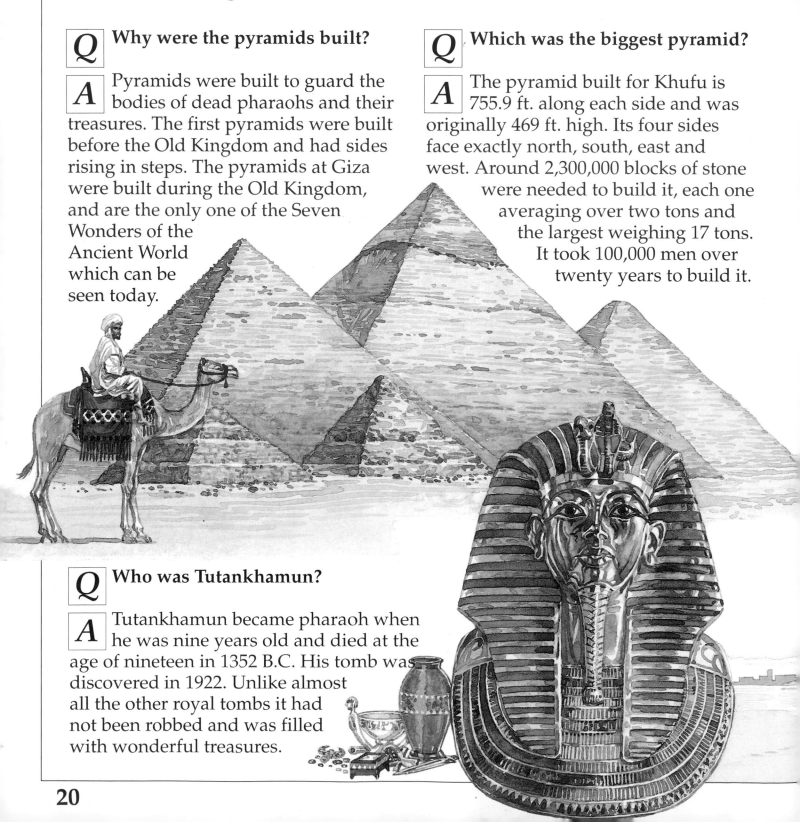

Q How did the Egyptians write?

A The Egyptians wrote in hieroglyphs, which were pictures of objects but could also be used to represent sounds. There were over 700 hieroglyphs.

Q What is the Rosetta Stone?

A The Rosetta Stone is a carved stone tablet with an inscription in Greek and hieroglyphic writing. It helped experts to understand hieroglyphics.

Q Is the Nile still important?

A The Nile is still vital to Egypt. Over ninety percent of the people still live along its banks or in its delta. The annual flood is now controlled by the High Dam at Aswan. This allows the water to be used more efficiently and some has been diverted for farming. The dam also generates electricity for industry.

Q What are the main sites that visitors can see?

A Near the ruins of Thebes are the temples of Luxor and Karnak, linked by an avenue of sphinxes 1.8 mi. long. On the south side of the Nile lies the "Valley of the Kings," where Tutankhamun's tomb was found. At Abu Simbel, near the border with Sudan, two massive temples in honor of Ramesses II were cut out of a sandstone cliff.

Who were the Greeks?

The Greeks lived in separate city states, scattered from southern Russia to Spain. Greek civilization flourished between 800 B.C. and 500 B.C. By 30 B.C. the Romans had taken over the Greek Empire.

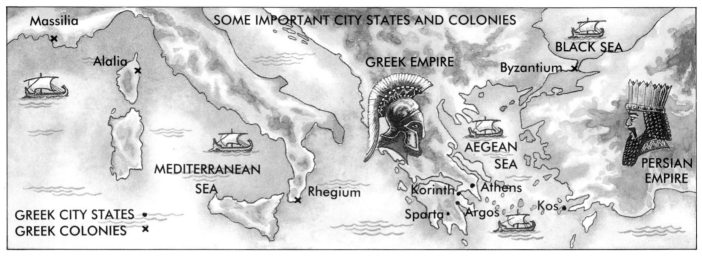

SOME IMPORTANT CITY STATES AND COLONIES

Massilia

Alalia

BLACK SEA

GREEK EMPIRE

Byzantium ×

MEDITERRANEAN SEA

AEGEAN SEA

PERSIAN EMPIRE

Rhegium

Korinth

Athens

Sparta   Argos

Kos

GREEK CITY STATES •
GREEK COLONIES ×

Q **What was a city state?**

A Each city state consisted of a city and the land surrounding it. They had their own government, army and money system. Most of them were situated near the sea and traded with each other.

Q **Which were the most important city states?**

A The leading city state was Athens. Athens had rich silver mines, a big navy and factories making things such as weapons, furniture, pottery and leather goods. The main rival to Athens was Sparta. Sparta was a warlike city state where every citizen served in the army.

Q **How big was Athens?**

A Athens had a territory of about 617 sq. mi. and a population of around 200,000. Only about 40,000 of these were free men, who fought in the army and took part in government. The rest were women, children, slaves and foreigners, all of whom had fewer rights than the Athenian men.

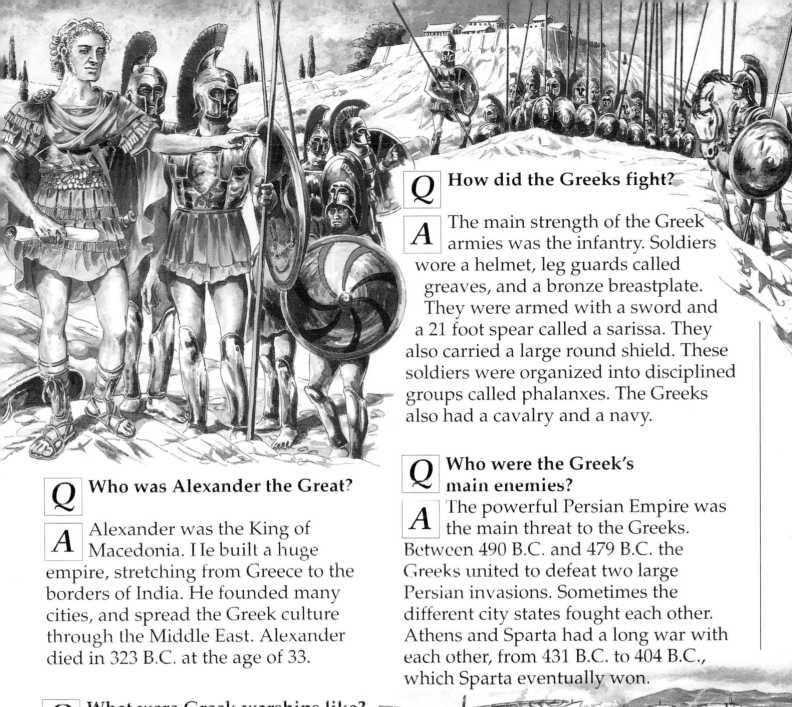

Q How did the Greeks fight?

A The main strength of the Greek armies was the infantry. Soldiers wore a helmet, leg guards called greaves, and a bronze breastplate. They were armed with a sword and a 21 foot spear called a sarissa. They also carried a large round shield. These soldiers were organized into disciplined groups called phalanxes. The Greeks also had a cavalry and a navy.

Q Who was Alexander the Great?

A Alexander was the King of Macedonia. He built a huge empire, stretching from Greece to the borders of India. He founded many cities, and spread the Greek culture through the Middle East. Alexander died in 323 B.C. at the age of 33.

Q Who were the Greek's main enemies?

A The powerful Persian Empire was the main threat to the Greeks. Between 490 B.C. and 479 B.C. the Greeks united to defeat two large Persian invasions. Sometimes the different city states fought each other. Athens and Sparta had a long war with each other, from 431 B.C. to 404 B.C., which Sparta eventually won.

Q What were Greek warships like?

A The most powerful warship was the trireme, which had three rows of oars, rowed by 170 men. It used sails when possible, but used its oars during calm weather or when it was going to ram another ship with its 9.8 ft. ram. It could travel at up to 9 mph.

The Greeks used inflated pig's bladders to play football.

Lots of writers used to live in Athens, so much is known about the way people lived at this time.

Q Did people eat well?

A Greek food was plain but healthy - fish, barley bread, goat's cheese, olives, figs, fruit, vegetables and salads flavored with parsley or basil. Meat was only eaten at festivals. Poor people ate lupins, a kind of flower, and grasshoppers.

Q What did Greeks learn at school?

A Apart from teaching how to read and write, schools also taught poetry, music and physical education. The Greeks thought that the ideal man should be able to fight, make speeches and entertain his friends. Girls did not go to school but learned how to spin and weave from their mothers.

Q How did women live?

A Women in Athens played little part in public life, except at religious festivals. They got married at age 13 or 14 and spent most of their time at home. They were allowed to own clothes, jewels and slaves; but not land or houses. Women in Sparta were treated equally to men and could own land, but they did not fight in the army.

Q How did people travel?

A Donkeys were used to carry people and goods short distances. As Greece is so mountainous it was usually easier to travel longer distances by boat around the coast rather than go overland.

Q What sort of religion did the Greeks have?

A The Greeks worshipped many gods and their greatest buildings were temples put up in honor of the gods. Only priests were allowed inside the temples. Sacrifices and other ceremonies were held outside.

Q What did people wear?

A The main item of clothing that men and women wore was the tunic. They also wore woolen cloaks, straw hats and leather sandals. Rich Greeks could afford silk clothes and expensive dyes to color their clothes, but most people wore lightweight linen and woolen clothes. Brooches and pins were used to hold clothes in place as buttons were not used.

Q What gods did they worship?

A The Greeks believed that the gods lived on Mount Olympus, the highest mountain in Greece. The most powerful god was Zeus, king of the gods. There were gods or goddesses for every aspect of life, such as war, love, music and hunting.

Zeus

Athena

Hera

Hermes

Only men were allowed to act in Greek plays. All actors wore masks.

Greek culture has had a lasting effect on later European history, in both the arts and sciences.

Q Did the Greeks make any scientific discoveries?

A The Greeks developed the scientific ideas that they discovered in Babylon and Egypt. For example, they knew that the Earth traveled around the Sun. They also invented steam engines. The ideas of Pythagoras and Euclid are still taught today.

Q What was the importance of Greek art and architecture?

A The Greek style of building was copied by the Romans and has been used by architects ever since, especially for public buildings, such as museums and town halls. Greek buildings were often decorated with bronze or marble statues. Many of these statues can be seen in museums all around the world.

Q Did the Greeks have myths and legends?

A The Greeks had many stories about heroes, such as Herakles (Hercules). There are also many stories about monsters, like the bull-headed Minotaur, the one-eyed Cyclops and the Gorgon, called Medusa, who could turn people to stone. These stories have been retold ever since Greek times.

The Greeks dated their history from 776 B.C., when the first Olympics were held.

Q How did the Greeks cure their sick?

A The Greeks were one of the first peoples to cure the sick using herbs, baths, exercise and diet rather than rely on so-called magic spells. Hippocrates of Kos (460-357 B.C.) is the most famous of all the Greek doctors. His ideas were still being studied 2,000 years after his death.

Q Did the Greeks go to the theater?

A The theater was very popular in Ancient Greece. The theater at Epidaurus could seat 14,000 people. "Drama," "theatre," "comedy," "chorus," "scenery," "tragedy" and "orchestra" are all originally Greek words. Many Greek plays by Athenian writers such as Sophokles are still put on today.

Q Did the Greeks play sports?

A The Greeks took sports very seriously. Running, wrestling and throwing the javelin were good training for war. Festivals, called games, were held every four years at four separate sites around Greece. The games at Olympia were the most important. The competitions included poetry and music as well as athletics. Only men were allowed into the games The modern Olympics were based on these games and were first held in Athens in 1896.

How big was the Roman Empire?

The Roman Empire covered all of the Mediterranean, much of Europe and even north Africa. It began around 753 B.C. and lasted over one thousand years.

Q Who founded Rome?

A According to Roman legend the twins Romulus and Remus founded Rome. As babies they were left to die, but were saved and cared for by wolves. The legend says they founded Rome in 753 B.C., with Romulus naming the city after himself and becoming the first king. However, historians think that the first kings were probably Etruscans who founded the city on the seven hills by the Tiber River in the seventh century B.C.

Q Who were the Etruscans?

A Very little is known about the Etruscans as their language is still not properly understood. Originally, they came from Turkey, and were at their height of power around 550 B.C. They were an advanced civilization which, amongst other things, wore robes like Roman togas and built the first drains in Rome.

Q How did Rome grow?

A At first Rome was only a weak city state. The Romans built a wall around the seven hills to defend themselves and built up a strong army. By 264 B.C. they had conquered all of Italy.

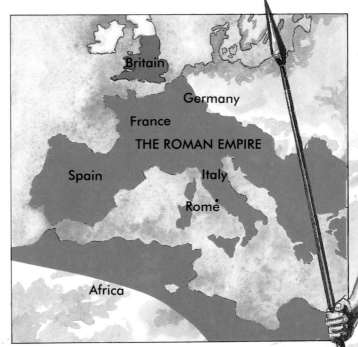

Q What were the Punic Wars?

A Rome's expansion brought it into conflict with the empire of Carthage (see page 12). Between 264 B.C. and 146 B.C. Rome fought three long wars with Carthage ending in total victory for Rome. In the course of these wars Rome conquered Sicily, Sardinia, Corsica, Spain and southern France.

All Roman roads had milestones which measured the distance from the city of Rome.

Q Why was the Roman army important?

A The army conquered Rome's empire and defended it against its enemies. The main strength of the army was the infantry who often won against much larger numbers because they were so well armed, trained and disciplined. They were also good at building fortifications and besieging cities.

Q Why were Roman roads important?

A The Romans built excellent roads which allowed their soldiers to move quickly between forts and boundaries. Merchants also used the roads, so trade flourished. There were over 52,800 mi. of roads which were so well built that they lasted for centuries.

Julius Caesar

Q Who was Julius Caesar?

A Julius Caesar was a famous general who conquered most of France. He was also a good public speaker and was popular with Romans. He made himself ruler of Rome, but was murdered by former friends who thought that Rome should be a republic and not ruled by one man.

Julius Caesar changed the calendar from 355 days a year to the 365-day system we use now.

What was life like in Rome?

A million people lived in Rome in A.D. 200. However, not everyone was well off. By A.D. 270, around 300,000 people were unemployed and lived on free handouts of barley bread, pork fat and olive oil from the government.

Q What did people eat?

A Rich Romans ate ham from Gaul or oysters from Britannia and spiced their food with pepper from India or ginger from China. Rice, sugar and carrots were known of but rarely eaten. Sheep and goat's milk was preferred to cow's milk. Poor people ate bean soup.

Q What were their homes like?

A Poor people lived in badly-built apartment blocks without bathrooms or kitchens. They used public baths and got hot food from cook-shops. The houses of rich Romans faced inwards on to an open space, called an atrium, with arcades to provide shade from the hot sun. Rich people often had big villas and estates in the country.

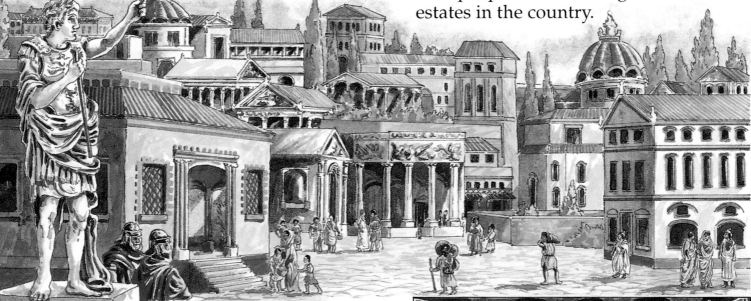

Q How did people keep clean and healthy?

A All Roman cities had public baths, like modern leisure centers, where people could bathe and swim. Romans also visited the baths to work out at the gymnasium, watch acrobats, gamble or chat with friends and buy snacks.

The Romans introduced football to Britain in A.D. 200.

Q Who did all the work?

A Nearly one third of the population were slaves, who did all the work. If they were educated they might have a comfortable life as a tutor, book keeper, doctor, or musician with a wealthy family. However, farmers, laborers and miners had a hard life and usually a short one.

Q What entertainments were there?

A As slaves did most of the work, many Roman citizens had time for leisure. Like the Greeks, they enjoyed the theater. The word "pantomime" comes from the Roman word for a mimed show. Even more popular were games which included chariot racing and combats in which gladiators fought each other or wild beasts.

Q What did the Romans believe in?

A The Romans adopted many Greek gods. They called Zeus "Jupiter," Poseidon "Neptune," Hermes "Mercury," and Aphrodite "Venus." Emperors were worshipped as gods after their death. When they came to live in a colony such as Britain, they often added in local gods as well. Romans also believed in household spirits, and in fortune telling through astrology, dice, palm reading, sacrifices and interpreting natural events, like lightning or flocks of birds.

Q How were people punished?

A The Romans had a very complicated system of law. Punishments for law breaking or minor offences, included fines or whipping . Major crimes might lead to loss of citizenship, banishment to a distant place or being sent to work in a mine or as a galley slave. Execution might be by beheading, drowning, crucifixion or being made to fight in the games. Prisons were only used to detain people until they were punished in some other way.

Roman rule had its greatest impact in northwest Europe, where Romans built the first cities and roads. Roman rule had less impact in Greece, Egypt and the Middle East where there were already long established civilizations.

Q What was the importance of Roman architecture?

A Until the 1100s all major buildings, such as churches, were based on Roman designs. Their rounded arch style is called "Romanesque." Interest in Roman architecture was renewed around 1500 during the period known as the Renaissance.

Q What effect did Roman rule have on Europe?

A Many of the main roads in Europe still follow the lines of old Roman roads. Also, many place names are linked to their Roman past. For example place names in England ending in -caster or -chester come from "castra," the Latin word for a military camp or fort.

Q How did Roman rule affect Christianity?

A Roman emperors often persecuted Christians because they refused to worship them as gods. However the emperor, Constantine, had a Christian mother, and Christianity then became the official religion of the empire.

Q Why was Latin important?

A After Roman rule had ended Latin was used as the written language of learning, government and religion throughout most of Europe for a thousand years. Over the same period Latin as a spoken language developed into Italian, French, Spanish, Portugese and Romanian. English, which developed from German, has thousands of words from Latin.

Q How has Roman history inspired art and literature?

A Roman history has inspired artists and historians for centuries. Shakespeare wrote the plays *Julius Ceasar* and *Antony and Cleopatra* a thousand years after the Romans left Britain. More recently the nineteenth century novels *Quo Vadis* and *The Last Days of Pompeii* have been made into films.

Q Where can Roman remains be seen today?

A Impressive ruins can be seen in most of the countries around the Mediterranean Sea. The Colosseum and Pantheon are two of the most impressive ruins in Rome. Pompeii, a Roman town, was preserved under a layer of volcanic ash when Mount Vesuvius erupted in A.D. 79. There are also many important remains in Britain such as Hadrian's Wall and Fishbourne Villa.

33

What is a warrior?

Warriors were men or women who fought bravely. Often they were not paid to fight, but fought because they believed they were right.

Warriors did not win all of the time. Some of the most famous warriors are those who lost, but who fought with great courage.

Byrhtnoth was an English earl. In 991, he and all his men died fighting a Viking force near Maldon in Essex. They fought so bravely that a poem, called "The Battle of Maldon," was written about their heroic struggle.

Shaka was the king of the Zulu, a large tribe in South Africa. In 1816, Shaka trained the Zulu warriors in new battle tactics. By 1850 the Zulus had defeated all neighboring tribes. In 1879 the Zulus wiped out a British regiment before being defeated by the British at Rorke's Drift and Kambula.

Warriors used different types of **weapons**. Early warriors used clubs and rocks, while more modern warriors used rifles and cannons.

The Assyrians conquered a large empire in the Near East about 3,000 years ago

Ashanti warriors fought in the dense forests of West Africa about 100 years ago.

The **Maori** live in New Zealand. They used to live in great tribes which fought wars with each other, and later, with European settlers. Sometimes whole tribes were killed in battle as they refused to surrender. Although the Europeans accepted the Maori as equals in 1840, wars continued for many years.

Alexander the Great

In 336 B.C. Alexander the Great became King of Macedonia (in northern Greece). He was only 20 years old. Within 13 years he had become the most powerful ruler in the world.

He defeated armies larger than his own using clever new tactics and weapons.

Alexander's horse was called **Bucephalus**. According to legend, Alexander, who was only 12 years old at the time, was the only person who could control him. When Bucephalus died Alexander named a town in India, Bucephala, in honor of him.

The Battle of Gaugamela in 331 B.C. was Alexander's greatest victory. He defeated a Persian army of 150,000 men with his army of only 35,000 Macedonians. The battle was won when Alexander led a cavalry charge which scattered the Persian infantry.

The cavalry led the attacks in battle. They were used to open gaps in the enemy army. The horsemen would charge forward, followed by the infantry.

King Darius, was Alexander's biggest enemy. He became ruler of the Persian Empire in 336 B.C. after murdering the previous three rulers. Darius was a successful warrior who defeated many enemies, but he lost two major battles to Alexander. In 330 B.C. Darius was murdered by his cousin.

Infantry in Alexander's army used a very long spear called a **sarissa**. Each sarissa was 15 feet long.

By 323 B.C. Alexander's Empire was the largest in the world at that time. He wanted to join all the kingdoms he had conquered to form one country. After Alexander died, his generals divided the empire between themselves. Within 150 years the empire no longer existed.

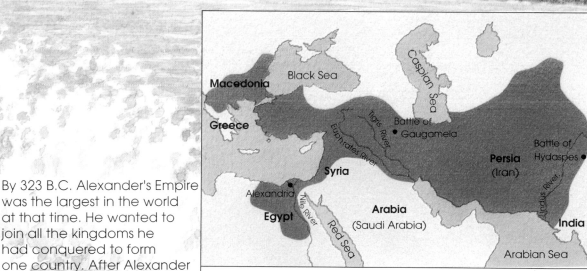

The Empire of Alexander the Great

Alexander reached **India** in 326 B.C. He defeated a local king, Porus, at the Battle of the Hydaspes (modern-day Jhelum) and added new territories to his empire.

Attila the Hun

Attila was the king of the Huns, a warlike tribe feared in Europe and Asia. He became sole King in 444 after murdering his elder brother, Breda, who was joint King at the time.

Attila organized the Huns into a powerful army. By conquering neighboring kingdoms he built up a large empire. Soon, he became known as "the scourge of God."

The Huns came from central Asia in about 370 and settled in what is now Hungary. Attila led his tribe in wars that ranged across Greece, southern Russia, Germany and France.

The Huns loved gold - during one raid into Greece they stole over 2,000 lbs!

In 453 Attila died suddenly after a feast on his wedding day. He was buried with his treasure. The slaves who buried him were all killed to keep the location secret. Without Attila's leadership, the Huns were easily defeated by their enemies.

Attila arrived in Italy in 452 and captured many cities. Pope Leo I persuaded him to spare Rome from attack.

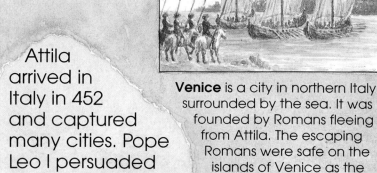

Venice is a city in northern Italy surrounded by the sea. It was founded by Romans fleeing from Attila. The escaping Romans were safe on the islands of Venice as the Huns did not have a navy.

Horses were the Huns' most important possession. They used them to look after their large herds of cattle and sheep. They also fought on horseback, using spears and bows to attack their enemies.

Hun warriors scarred their faces with knives to make themselves look fierce to frighten their enemies.

The Huns used the **lasso** as a weapon. One Hun would catch an enemy with a lasso, allowing another warrior to kill the captive.

The Roman Empire began around 753 B.C. and lasted over 1,000 years until A.D. 476. It covered all the lands around the Mediterranean, and much of Europe.

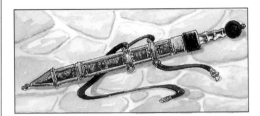

These lands were conquered and policed by the Roman Army. The Romans defeated many enemies because of their superior weapons and tactics.

The Romans were excellent builders as well as warriors. They made roads to move their armies from one place to another, and built forts and walls to keep out invaders. **Hadrian's Wall**, in northern England, was built to keep enemies from invading England from Scotland.

The legionary was the most important type of Roman warrior. Legionaries wore strong suits of armor and fought on foot. They were grouped together in a century, made up of 80 legionaries led by an officer known as a centurion.

Roman legionaries marched and fought together in a large group of 5,200 legionaries, called a **legion**.

Horatius was a legendary early Roman warrior. In about 670 B.C. a large Etruscan army (from northern Italy) attacked Rome. The bridge leading to Rome across the Tiber River had to be cut down to stop the Etruscan invasion. Horatius fought the Etruscans single-handedly to give the Romans time to cut down the bridge. Rome was saved and Horatius survived to be declared a hero.

Mark Antony was a famous general. He fell in love with Cleopatra, the Queen of Egypt, and gave her land belonging to Rome. This led to a civil war with the Roman authorities which Mark Antony lost. Later, he took his own life.

Legionaries arranged themselves in special formations when attacking the enemy. The "tortoise" protected legionaries from arrows and spears. The "wedge" was used to smash through enemy ranks.

A bronze eagle was the symbol of a legion and it was carried into battle. Romans thought it was an insult to the gods if the eagle were captured by the enemy.

The Roman Empire was very large and had many enemies. There were tribes fighting their Roman conquerors, and armies from other empires trying to invade Rome.

The **Celts** were divided into many different tribes, who lived right across Europe from Scotland to Serbia. They were often a war-like people, who rode chariots into battle and sometimes sang as they fought. After a battle, the Celts would cut off the heads of their dead enemies and hold a feast to celebrate.

Vercingetorix was the Celtic leader of Gaul (modern-day France). He fought against the Roman general Julius Caesar in 52 B.C. After several battles, Vercingetorix was captured and beheaded.

Hannibal was a famous nobleman from Carthage (in modern-day Tunisia). He was one of Rome's most dangeous enemies. In 218 B.C. he led his army, along with 38 elephants, from Spain through France and across the Alps into Italy. He won many battles there, including the defeat of 50,000 Romans at Cannae. He never reached Rome and was forced to return to Carthage.

Spartacus was a slave who escaped from a gladiator school in 73 B.C. Thousands of other slaves ran away to join him. Spartacus led them through Italy stealing and burning everything they could find. He was defeated and died in battle at Lucania in 71 B.C. The 6,000 prisoners captured by the Romans were all crucified.

Boudicca was Queen of the Iceni, a tribe from East Anglia, in England. In A.D. 61 she led her tribe in revolt after she and her daughters had been ill-treated by the Romans, who had also increased the taxes. Boudicca's Celtic warriors destroyed Colchester, London and St. Albans before being beaten by the Romans. Rather than surrender, she poisoned herself.

Arminius was a German chief. In A.D. 9 he and his warriors trapped three Roman legions in a swampy forest and killed them all.

Masada was a fortress in Palestine held by 1,000 Jewish rebels in A.D. 72-73. After a two-year siege by 15,000 Romans, all but seven of the Jews, including the children, committed suicide rather than surrender.

Ireland was never conquered by the Romans. Instead, Ireland remained a land ruled by Celtic chiefs.

Although there was a High King of Ireland most tribes continued to fight each other.

Irish kings and chiefs often lived in well defended **strongholds**. The remains of the Rock of Cashel in Tipperary County are a good example of an ancient Irish stronghold. The rock was home to the kings of Munster.

Cuchulainn was the great warrior hero of Ulster. His story is told in a poem called "The Cattle Raid of Cooley" which was written around the year 500. In the poem Cuchulainn is described as being very strong and having a terrible temper.

Brian Boru was the greatest High King of Ireland, reigning from 1002 to 1014. He fought to free Ireland from Viking invaders. He was murdered by a fleeing band of Vikings after finally defeating the Viking army at Clontarf.

Women are important characters in Irish mythology. The legendary **Queen Maeve** of Connaught led an army against Ulster, and fought against Cuchulainn.

Fionn mac Cumhaill was the legendary hero of Leinster. According to the stories told about him, he led a band of brave young warriors who loved to hunt. These warriors were known as the Fianna. The Fianna rebelled against Cairbre, High King of Ireland, in an argument about hunting lands. The Fianna were destroyed in the following battle.

Strongbow was the nickname of Richard Fitzgilbert, a Norman lord. He came to Ireland in 1170 to help Dermot MacMurrogh, King of Leinster, become High King. After Dermot's death, Strongbow grabbed his lands for himself. Soon, other Norman and English knights came to Ireland and took over much of the country.

Vikings

The Vikings came from Norway, Denmark and Sweden. They raided northern Europe and even traveled to North America and Italy.

A carved head from a Viking ship

The Vikings were also merchants, trading with Arabs and people from Asia. They sold furs, ivory and slaves and bought silk, spices and gold.

Weapons were made by skilled craftspeople. Axes and swords were favorite weapons. Valuable swords were passed from father to son. They were given frightening names such as "blood-sucker" or "man-killer!"

Raids were carried out by warriors in longships. As many as 100 longships would take part in a single raid. The Vikings would land, capture as much money, food, cattle and valuables as possible and sail away again.

Longships were narrow boats which could be up to 100 feet in length. They were not very heavy and were very quick through the water as they had oars as well as a large sail. Some longships had dragon heads carved on to them to make them look fiercer.

Sweyn Forkbeard was the greatest Viking of his time. He built a large empire based around the North Sea. He was King of Denmark and Norway, and in 1013 he became King of England.

The Vikings started to settle in the places that they had raided in the past. There were **settlements** in northern England, northern France and southern Ireland. Remains of these settlements can still be seen in York, in England, and Dublin, in Ireland.

Eric Bloodaxe became King of Northumberland, in England, in 948. He had been forced to flee from Norway after murdering two of his brothers to become sole King of Norway. Eric was driven out of England in 948, and again in 954. He was killed later that year on returning to England.

Viking warriors believed that when they died they would go to **Valhalla**, the banquet hall of the gods. Viking chiefs and famous warriors would often be buried with their boats and their favorite possessions when they died. Sometimes the body would be placed on the deck of the boat and burned.

Genghis Khan united all the Mongol tribes of central Asia and created the largest land empire the world has ever seen.

His empire relied upon ferocious mounted warriors and a reign of terror, which left cities burnt to the ground and millions of people dead.

Each warrior had two bows, 100 arrows, a lance and a sword. Arrows came in several designs. Some were specially shaped to travel long distances, others to pierce metal armor. One type of arrow was fitted with a whistle to frighten enemy troops.

Genghis Khan's real name was **Temujin**. He was born in 1167, the son of a minor tribal chief. His father was poisoned by a neighboring tribe, but Temujin became leader himself. He acted very bravely in battle and at a meeting of the Mongol tribes in 1206 he was given the title "Genghis Khan," which means "Great Ruler."

Genghis Khan was also the ruler of the **Merkit**, **Tartar**, **Kirghiz** and **Naiman** tribes.

The Mongols were a very ruthless tribe. When they captured a city they would put women, young children and the craftsmen who made weapons to one side. Then they would kill everybody else. When the city of **Merv** was captured, about 700,000 people were killed.

The invasion of **China** began in 1211 when the Mongols broke through the Great Wall. In 1215, Peking was captured and northern China was conquered.

The Mongols fought on horseback. Their horses were small and strong. They were bred to withstand the cold and heat and were trained to keep calm in battle.

The **Mongol Empire** was the largest land empire ever known. By 1279 it stretched from Hungary to Korea and included most of Asia.

Russia

Arabia

India

China

Pacific Ocean

Arabian Sea

◼ The Mongol Empire

Crusaders

The Crusades were wars between Christians and Muslims. There were seven Crusades between the years 1095 and 1300.

The name "Crusader" comes from the Latin word for cross. The Christian warriors were called Crusaders because they wore a cross as their badge.

Assassins were sent into Crusader camps by the Muslims to murder important leaders.

Richard the Lionheart was a King of England who led the Third Crusade in 1190. At the battle of Arsouf, in 1191, Richard defeated a large Muslim army and in the following year, he defeated another Muslim army at Jaffa. He led the Christian attack himself and acted with great bravery. Richard forced the Muslims to agree to a truce that allowed Christians to visit Jerusalem.

Warrior monks fought in the Crusades. These were special monks who made promises to God to fight against the Muslims. The Templar Order was the most famous group of warrior monks. The order was founded in 1118 to protect pilgrims going to Jerusalem. Other orders included the Hospitallers, the Trufac and the Teutonic.

Saladin was the great Muslim leader of the 1100s. In 1175 he became Sultan (ruler) of Damascus and went on to unite the Muslims. He defeated the Crusaders in many important battles and stopped them from taking over Jerusalem.

El Cid was the nickname given to Rodrigo di Vivar. He was a great Spanish warrior who fought against the Muslims. El Cid means "The Champion." In 1094 he defeated the Muslims and captured the city of Valencia. He ruled it until his death in battle in 1099.

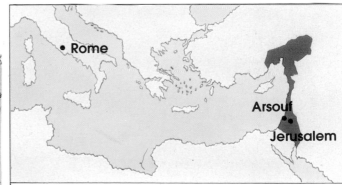

- Rome
- Arsouf
- Jerusalem

The Kingdom of Outremer

The Crusaders set up their own kingdom in Palestine called **Outremer**. The name means "Beyond the Sea," because Palestine is across the Mediterranean Ocean from Rome, the Christians' headquarters.

Aztecs and Incas

The Aztecs were a warlike people who lived in Mexico. By 1450, they had formed a large empire stretching from the Pacific Ocean to the Caribbean.

Aztec Empire

Inca Empire

The Incas came from Peru. Their empire covered an area four times as large as France. The Incas believed it was their holy duty to conquer other tribes and make them worship the Sun God.

The Aztecs and Incas used weapons made from wood with sharp polished pieces of a rock called **obsidian** set in them to make a cutting edge.

In 1423 Pachacuti, the Inca ruler, ordered work to start on the fortress of **Sacasahuaman**. The fortress had three massive towers and three walls made of stone. The walls were in a zigzag shape. The stones were specially shaped to fit into each other like pieces in a jigsaw.

Every Aztec man joined the **army** at the age of 17. If he had not performed a brave act by the age of 23, he had to leave the army to become a farmer or merchant. Very brave warriors were allowed to wear special animal skins.

Spanish troops, known as **Conquistadors** (meaning conquerors), attacked the Aztecs in 1519, and the Incas in 1532. The Conquistadors rode horses into battle and were armed with steel swords and guns. These modern weapons were too powerful for the Aztecs and Incas, and both their empires were conquered.

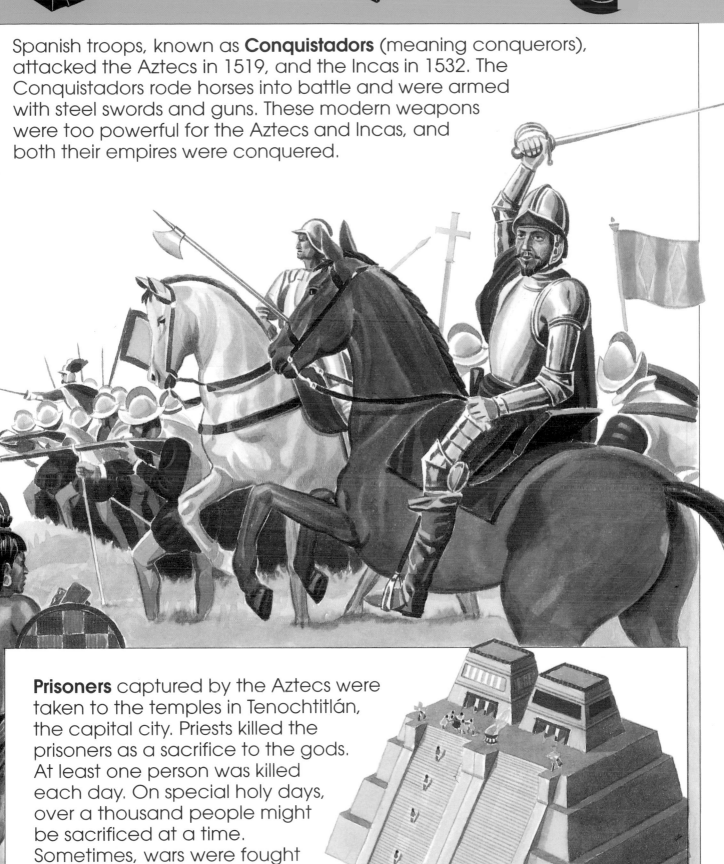

Prisoners captured by the Aztecs were taken to the temples in Tenochtitlán, the capital city. Priests killed the prisoners as a sacrifice to the gods. At least one person was killed each day. On special holy days, over a thousand people might be sacrificed at a time. Sometimes, wars were fought simply to capture prisoners.

Sitting Bull was the greatest leader of the Sioux people. He united the Sioux tribes.

With the help of the Blackfeet, Cheyenne and Arapahoe tribes, he led a war against the American settlers.

Warriors like the Sioux fought on horseback. They were armed with spears, bows and arrows, or guns bought from the white settlers.

The **first Indian War** began in 1608 when English settlers fought the Powhatan tribe in Virginia. The war ended in 1613 when the Indian princess Pocahontas married an Englishman.

Red Cloud was chief of one of the Sioux tribes. He fought against the American army to stop them from building forts and a road across land belonging to the Sioux and Cheyenne tribes. The war lasted for two years, from 1865 until 1867, when the government was forced to leave the tribes' land. Red Cloud made peace with the settlers, but continued to defend the rights of his people with many visits to the government in Washington.

When **gold** was found on Sioux land, the American government ordered Sitting Bull to move his people to a new reservation 235 mi. away. Sitting Bull refused to move and war broke out between the government and the Sioux.

In 1876, General Custer was sent with the 7th Cavalry to attack the Indian camp at **Little Big Horn**. Custer sent part of his troops to attack the Indian rear, and charged forward with the remaining troops. He rode straight into a trap set by Sitting Bull and another chief, called Crazy Horse. Custer and all his men were killed.

Geronimo was the leader of the Apache, who lived in the deserts of the U.S.-Mexico border. In 1859, the Apache were attacked by Mexicans. After this the Apache fought a war against all whites. For many years Geronimo led his warriors in a brutal conflict until he surrendered in 1886.

The Orient is the name given to the lands to the east of the Mediterranean Sea, especially those in eastern Asia, such as China or Japan.

Many ruthless warriors have fought each other across this vast area of land.

Samurai warriors came from Japan. They were highly trained fighters who were loyal to their local lord. All Samurai followed a strict set of rules, known as Bushido. These rules encouraged the Samurai to be brave, honest and live a simple life. If a Samurai broke the rules of Bushido or lost a batle, he had to kill himself. This was known as seppuku.

The **Great Wall of China** was built by the Emperor Shih Huang-ti around 220 B.C. It was designed to protect China from invasions from the north. It is over 3,728 mi. long and wide enough to drive a chariot along the top. Today it is a major tourist attraction.

Early Chinese armies were made up of large numbers of peasants. They fought on foot as only the nobles could afford chariots or proper weapons. By 200 B.C. the Han Emperors had introduced cavalry. An example of what warriors looked like at this time can now be seen at Xian in China after the discovery of 6,000 life-size terracotta models of the Emperor Shih Huang-ti's army.

Timur the Lame, or Tamerlane as he was known in Europe, was the ruthless leader of the Tartar warriors from southern Asia. He was born in 1336 in Samarkand, which is in modern-day Tajikistan. By 1399, he had conquered or made treaties with all of central Asia, and invaded Russia and India. Timur was a cruel person who slaughtered thousands of people. He would build great pyramids of skulls from the people he killed before taking their treasure back to Samarkand.

An Lu-Shan was a Turkish warrior who became ruler of China. As a young man, he was a cavalry commander in the Chinese army. He won many victories against the enemies of China and was soon commander of the entire northern army. In 756, thinking the Emperor had ordered his death, An Lu-Shan attacked China. He overthrew the Emperor and became ruler of China. He was murdered one year later by a servant.

Freedom fighters are warriors who try to free their country from the rule of a foreign nation.

Most freedom fighters work in small groups rather than with a large army. Sometimes they win and their country is freed. Other freedom fighters fail but they become heroes and inspire others to follow their ideas.

Joan of Arc led the French in a war against the English. In 1429 England ruled most of France. Joan, a young farmer's daughter, persuaded the Dauphin (the French heir to the throne) to let her fight with a small army. Joan amazed the troops with her bravery and leadership. She was captured and executed by the English in 1431. Thousands of French people were inspired by Joan and within a few years France was free.

Simon Bolívar fought to free South Americans from the Spanish Empire. In 1810 Venezuela threw out the Spanish governor. Bolivar took command of the rebel army and won many victories. In 1821 Spain accepted defeat. Bolívar then went on to lead rebels in Colombia, Peru, Ecuador and Bolivia.

Francois Toussaint L'Ouverture was a black slave who led the slaves of Haiti to freedom. In 1791 he led a slave revolt against the foreign rulers of the island and by 1797 he was ruler of Haiti. Toussant outlawed slavery and brought in many humane laws.

Giuseppe Garibaldi led a small group of Italians to try and unite Italy. In 1860 Italy was made up of a large number of small kingdoms and much of the country was controlled by Austria. Garibaldi led just 1,000 men (called the "Redshirts" due to the color of their clothes) to Sicily. He began a revolution and swept northward overthrowing many rulers. After only six months most of Italy joined together under the rule of the King of Piedmont.

Robert the Bruce led the Scots against the English. In 1296 Edward I of England was crowned King of Scotland. Robert the Bruce, a great grandson of an earlier Scottish king, claimed that he should be king. For years he was unsuccessful, until the Battle of Bannockburn in 1314, where the English army was smashed by Robert's Scottish troops. Scotland was a free nation again.

Mythical warriors appear in legends from many countries.

Although fantastic stories are told about these warriors, the legends are often based upon the lives of real people.

Gilgamesh was a legendary hero of Ancient Persia in about 2000 B.C. In the legend, Gilgamesh was a king who goes on a long journey to try to discover the meaning of life. It is thought that Gilgamesh was a famous warrior-king of Uruk in about 2500 B.C.

Horus was an Ancient Egyptian god. It is thought that the many stories told about his conflict with the god Seth refer to ancient tribal conflicts before the first pharaoh united Egypt in about 2800 B.C.

The Ancient Greeks and Persians told stories of female warriors called **Amazons**. The Amazons were a race of war-like women who raided other countries to capture gold and men. In fact, the Amazon legend was probably based on a real-life tribe called Sarmatians, who lived near the Black Sea between 800 B.C. and 300 B.C. Sarmatian women had equal rights with men and fought in battles. This seemed very strange to the Greeks and Persians of the time and led to the stories about the Amazons.

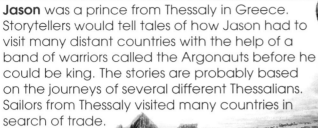

Jason was a prince from Thessaly in Greece. Storytellers would tell tales of how Jason had to visit many distant countries with the help of a band of warriors called the Argonauts before he could be king. The stories are probably based on the journeys of several different Thessalians. Sailors from Thessaly visited many countries in search of trade.

King Arthur is a legendary warrior of Britain. According to legend, Arthur was a great king who led a band of noble and gentle knights. The knights sat around a round table so that no one would appear to be more important than any of the others by sitting at the head of the table. In fact, Arthur was probably a Celtic warrior who fought against the Anglo-Saxons (who invaded Britain after the Romans left). He is thought to have been killed at the Battle of Camlann in about 515.

Sigurd was a great hero warrior of the Vikings. He was the last of the Volsung tribe and had many adventures, like fighting a dragon and finding treasure. Nobody has been able to discover who the character of Sigurd was based upon.

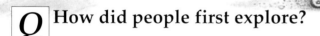

To frighten off other travelers, the Phoenicians spread tales of sea serpents.

Phoenicians ruled the Mediterranean for one thousand years from 1400 B.C.

The earliest explorers lived in pre-historic times, more than half a million years ago. They were Stone Age people in the land now called Africa, searching for new sources of food and shelter.

Q Why did people begin to explore?

A Exploration was often a question of survival. People hoped to find fresh supplies of food and living materials and often a safer place away from enemies.

Q What were the earliest boats made from?

A Boats might have been made from hollowed-out logs, reeds, or skins stretched over a wooden frame.

Q How did people first explore?

A The first explorers probably traveled on foot or on horseback. But it was easier to travel greater distances across the sea or along rivers by boat.

Q Who were the greatest early explorers to cross oceans?

A The Phoenicians, who lived in what is now Israel, built a large fleet of ships around 800 B.C. They traveled as far as Africa and the British Isles to trade.

Q What cargoes did ships carry?

A Egyptian ships carried wood, ivory, silver, gold, cloth and spices. They also carried animals.

Q Who first sailed around Africa?

A The dangerous journey around what is now called the Cape of Good Hope was made by the Phoenicians in about 600 B.C.

In about 1500 B.C., Queen Hatshepsut of Egypt sent five ships to Punt (now called Somalia) for spices, monkeys, dogs and minerals.

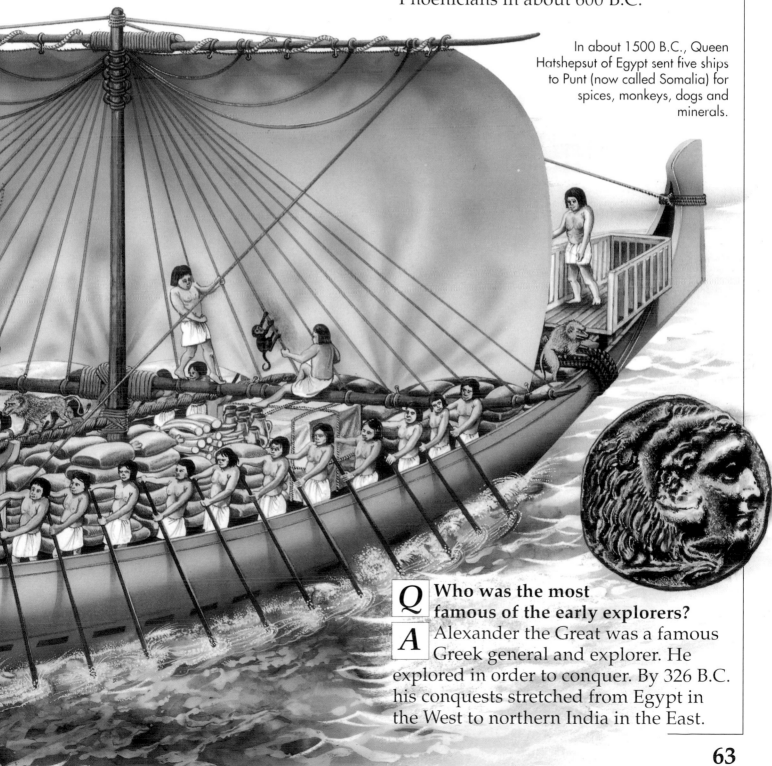

Q Who was the most famous of the early explorers?

A Alexander the Great was a famous Greek general and explorer. He explored in order to conquer. By 326 B.C. his conquests stretched from Egypt in the West to northern India in the East.

Viking sailors sometimes relied on the instinct of birds. From time to time they would release a raven and follow it, hoping it would lead them to

Before modern instruments such as radar and radio were invented, explorers had to use other methods to discover their position at sea and in strange lands.

About 3,000 years ago, Polynesians were exploring the Pacific Islands in canoes. To navigate they studied the positions of the stars, wind direction and the pattern of ocean waves.

Q How did the earliest explorers navigate?

A Navigators studied the position of the Moon, Sun and stars. Some also knew how to sail along a given latitude (distance north or south of a line called the Equator which runs around the middle of the Earth).

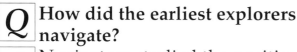

Q How did explorers find remote islands?

A Early sailors could guess where land lay from the behavior of sea creatures and from the shape and size of waves. Their boats may have been carried across the ocean by currents.

Q How did sailors know they were near land if they didn't have a chart?

A Sailors knew they were near land when they saw birds or floating vegetation. Sometimes the color of the sea or the shape of clouds changed near land.

The telescope was invented in the early seventeenth century.

Q Who invented the compass?

A The Chinese invented the first compass about 4,000 years ago. However, European explorers did not use them until about 1,000 years ago.

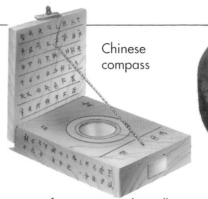

Chinese compass

A compass consists of a magnetized needle on a pivot. Because of the Earth's magnetism, the needle always points to magnetic north.

Early charts, called portulan charts, were drawn on stretched animal skin (parchment).

Q What were early charts like?

A In the fifteenth century, charts showed coastal features, ports and danger spots. Direction lines radiated out from compass points to help seamen follow a direct course from one place to another.

Q What was a quadrant used for?

A The quadrant was the earliest instrument used to measure the height of the Sun or stars. It was invented by the Arabs. In the fifteenth century, seamen used it to work out their latitude.

The sights of a quadrant were lined up with the Sun or a star. The plumb line showed the number of degrees above the horizon to work out a ship's position at sea.

Q What was an astrolabe?

A Like the quadrant, the astrolabe was used to work out latitude. Both instruments were fairly inaccurate at sea, when readings were taken on a rolling deck.

Astrolabes were made of brass. There were two holes at either end of the arm, which were lined up so the Sun or a star shone through. The arm then showed the height above the horizon.

How far did the Vikings travel?

Some Vikings dared to sail into the unknown Atlantic - to the Faroes, Iceland, Greenland and even America.

Longships were shallow in depth, so Vikings could sail a long way up rivers and estuaries.

The Viking Age began around A.D. 800 and lasted about three hundred years. Vikings explored many distant lands including parts of Russia and North America.

Q Why did the Vikings search for new lands?

A Scandinavia, where the Vikings came from, has long, cold winters and much of the land is difficult to farm. Large families could not grow enough food, so new places to live had to be found.

Q Which was the first Viking colony?

A The Vikings first discovered Iceland in A.D. 860 when a group of explorers were blown off course. Irish monks had already reached the island about sixty-five years earlier.

Q What were Viking ships like?

A Vikings warships were known as longships. These were fast, sleek ships, well suited to raiding and long-distance travel.

Cross-section of a longship

Q What goods did the Vikings traders want?

A They wanted gold, silver, spices, silk, jewelery and iron.

Q Where did the Vikings go?

A The Vikings raided France, Britain and Ireland. They sailed around Spain and into the Mediterranean. Vikings journeyed down the great rivers of Russia to reach the Caspian Sea and the Black Sea. They also crossed the Atlantic to North America.

Q Where did the crew sleep?

A There were no cabins on Viking ships. Viking sailors just covered themselves with animal hides or blankets, though some ships had awnings (roof-coverings). Voyages were not normally made in the coldest winter months .

Q Where did Vikings put their cargo?

A Viking ships did not have decks. Cargo was stored on the floor in the middle of the ship between the oarsmen who sat in the bow and stern.

Knarrs were probably no more than 60 ft. long.

On voyages Vikings ate smoked fish, dried meat and vegetables.

Q What were Viking cargo ships like?

A Vikings carried cargo in ships called knarrs, which were wider than longships and mostly used for coastal trading.

Arab merchants who traded with India and the Far East were incredibly rich.

Arabs played an important part in the history of exploration. In the sixth and seventh centuries they conquered a huge empire, spreading education and Islam.

Q What sort of ships did Arabs have?

A Arab ships were known as dhows. They had triangular sails, and needed only a small crew.

Q Where did Arab explorers learn about navigation?

A Arabs learned about navigation in the Indian Ocean while on trading missions. They worked out how to find their way by the stars. They also learned about tides, ocean currents and the monsoon cycle (heavy rainstorms).

Q Did Arab explorers make maps?

A Yes. There is a famous map of about 1150 made on a silver tablet by an explorer called Idrisi. He was a Spanish-born Arab who visited France and England as well as the East.

Early maps included only the top of Africa. The ship-like figure on the left is meant to show three lakes feeding into the River Nile.

Q Who was the greatest Arab explorer?

A The most famous Arab explorer was Ibn Batuta from Tangier in North Africa. He visited many countries from 1325 to 1355.

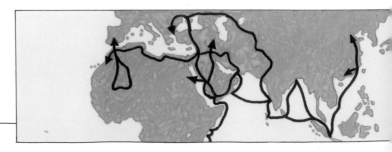

Stories about Arab merchants inspired many adventure stories, including *Sinbad the Sailor* and *The Thousand and One Nights*.

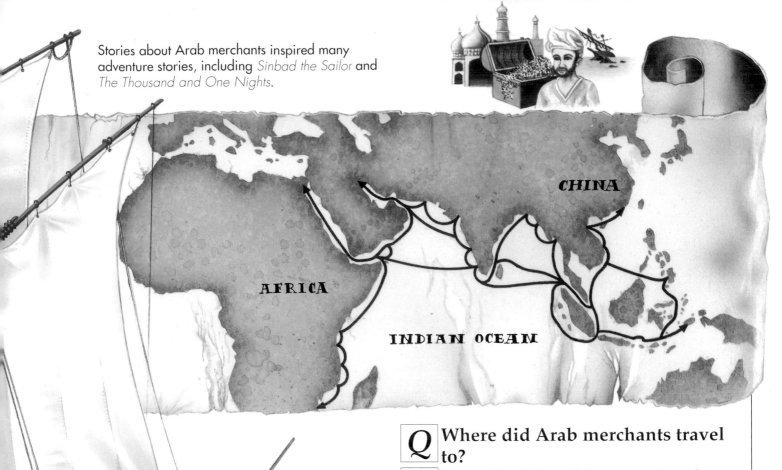

AFRICA

CHINA

INDIAN OCEAN

Dhows are still used in the Indian Ocean today.

Q **Where did Arab merchants travel to?**

A From the 7th to 9th centuries, they reached India, China, Russia, southern Africa and Zanzibar (Tanzania).

Q **How did European knowledge compare with that of the Arabs?**

A Europeans knew less about science, mathematics and geography than the Arabs. Their view of the world was restricted by Christian beliefs. On European maps the Earth was shown as a circle with Jerusalem at its center.

China Asia India
Tower of Babel
Europe
Jerusalem
Africa

Q **Was there any region where Arab explorers were afraid to go?**

A Arabs called the Atlantic "The Sea of Darkness." Idrisi may have sailed into it, but if he did he was the only Arab who dared to do so.

Q **How did the West come to share Arab learning?**

A Christian knights came into contact with the Arabs during the Crusades (1096-1291) when the Christians tried to win back Jerusalem. Arabs had also conquered much of Spain.

Ibn Batuta traveled about 74,500 mi. during his thirty years of voyages.

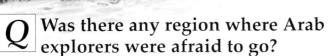

Marco Polo

Kublai Khan

Who first made contact with China?

China, in the Far East, was a difficult place to reach. In 1271 Marco Polo, the son of a merchant from Venice, Italy, traveled overland to Peking (Beijing) with his father and uncle and spent many years with the Chinese emperor Kublai Khan.

Q What did merchants want from the Chinese?

A Western merchants wanted silk, spices and porcelain which they traded in return for gold and silver.

Q Why did Marco Polo travel to China?

A Marco's father, Niccolo, and his uncle, Maffeo, had already spent fifteen years in China. They returned to Italy and then, in 1271, decided to go back, taking Marco with them. They carried gifts from Pope Gregory X, who hoped the great Mongol leader Kublai Khan would recognize Christianity as superior to the many other religions in China.

Q How long did Marco stay in the Khan's court?

A The Khan kept Marco at his court for seventeen years, sending him on diplomatic missions all over China. Because of his quick grasp of languages and his skill at making notes on everything he saw, Marco was able to report back to Kublai Khan and, later, to people in Venice.

Q Were the Polo family the first Europeans to reach China?

A No. The route known as the Silk Road, which ran from China to the West, had been used by traders since about 500 B.C., but the Polos were the first Europeans to travel its entire length and make contact with Chinese leaders.

Venice

The Silk Road

Q How did the Polos travel to Shangdu, where Kublai Khan had his palace?

A They used camels to carry provisions through Armenia into Persia (Iran), through Afghanistan, the Gobi Desert and China. They traveled 6,959 mi., and took three-and-a-half years to reach Shangdu. On the way they spent a year in Kanchow learning the customs of the Mongol peoples.

Junks were flat-bottomed ships with sails made of matting stiffened with wooden strips. They could make long voyages.

Q How did Marco return?

A Marco was given the job of escorting a princess to Persia (Iran), where she was to marry a prince. After stopping at Sumatra, Java, Malaya, Ceylon (Sri Lanka) and India, he delivered the princess to Persia and sailed home to Venice.

The Silk Road was so dangerous that goods were passed along it from one merchant to another. No one before had travelled its entire length.

Shang-tu

PERSIA

The Chinese had already explored to the west. In the second century B.C. they reached Persia (Iran).

CHINA

Canton

Hormuz

On his death bed, Marco Polo was asked to admit that he had been lying about his adventures. He replied "I have not told half of what I saw."

INDIA

——— The Silk Road
– – – Marco Polo's Route

AFRICA

Q What new sights did Marco see?

A On his travels Marco saw many strange and wonderful things unknown to Europeans. He marveled at the huge cities and strange-shaped ships on the great rivers. He saw, for the first time, people using paper money, burning coal not wood, and printing words on paper using wooden blocks. Marco also found sources of jewels and spices.

Q How did people learn of Marco's adventures?

A After Marco's return in 1295, war broke out between the Venetians and the Genoese, and he was taken prisoner. In prison he dictated his story to another prisoner. Many people did not believe his book, which described the discovery of oil, coal, magnificent palaces, parades of elephants, gifts to Kublai Khan of 100,000 white horses and huge jewels that were beyond the imagination of the Venetians.

The fifteenth and early sixteenth centuries are often called the Great Age of Exploration because so many discoveries were made at this time. Sea routes were found to the East, and unknown lands were explored - for example, America, the West Indies and the Pacific.

Q Why were there so many explorers at this time?

A This was an exciting time of new learning. Western Europeans wanted to find out more about the world, and had developed ships that would allow them to do so. Merchants wanted to obtain such valuable things as spices, silk, gems and fine china. Spices from the East were needed for cooking and medicines.

Q Which country began the Great Age of Exploration?

A The Portugese, in the early fifteenth century. Ships sailing out of Lisbon port picked up strong winds which drove them directly south until they picked up a wind to drive them east.

Q Who first sailed round the southern tip of Africa?

A The Portuguese captain, Bartolomeo Dias did, in 1487. He had two caravels and a larger ship to carry stores. He sailed round the Cape of Good Hope but his crew refused to go any further.

Q Who paid for the expeditions?

A Usually they were sponsored by the royal family of a country. Prince Henry of Portugal became known as Henry the Navigator not because he ever went to sea, but because he sponsored Portuguese expeditions. Spanish and English kings and queens also paid for explorers' voyages. They wanted to find riches overseas and to gain power over any new lands that were discovered.

Q Which European first reached India by sea?

A The Portuguese sailor, Vasco da Gama did. He followed Dias' route around Africa. Then he took on board an Arab pilot who helped him navigate to India. Da Gama lost two ships and half his men, but took back to Portugal a cargo of spices and precious gems.

Many of Da Gama's men died of scurvy from not having enough fresh food.

Caravels were quite small - only about 78 ft. long.

Q **What ships did the Portuguese use?**

A Caravels, which were small, strong, fast trading boats were used. They could sail into dangerous or shallow waters where larger ships could not go.

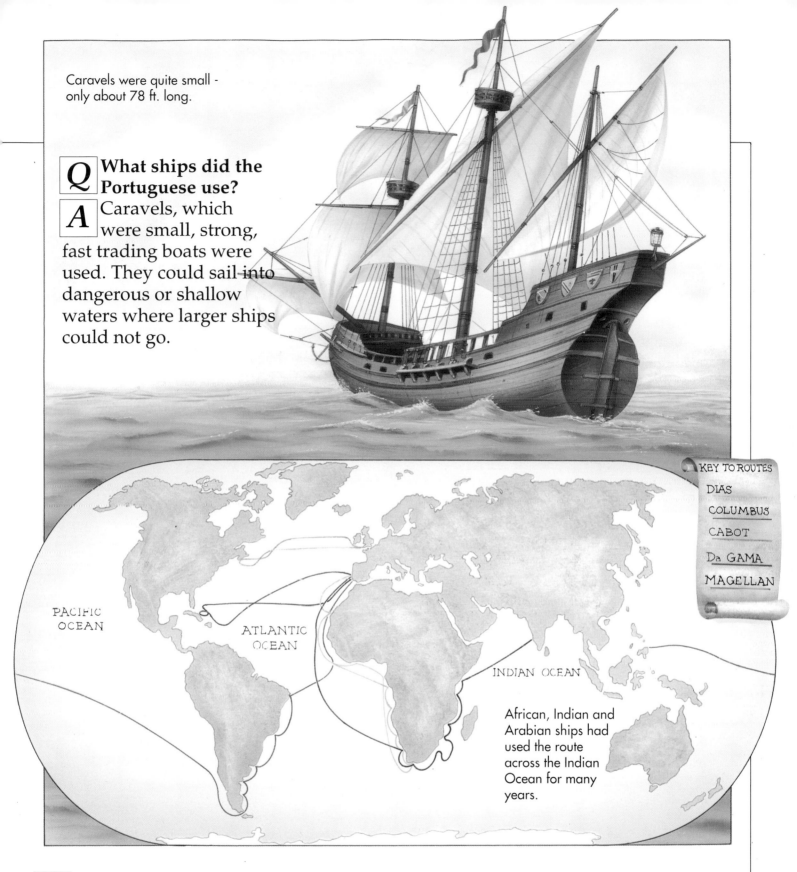

KEY TO ROUTES
DIAS
COLUMBUS
CABOT
Da GAMA
MAGELLAN

PACIFIC OCEAN

ATLANTIC OCEAN

INDIAN OCEAN

African, Indian and Arabian ships had used the route across the Indian Ocean for many years.

Q **Which were the most exciting years of the Great Age of Exploration?**

A A These major discoveries were made within the astonishingly short space of thirty-four years:

1487 Dias sailed around the tip of Africa.
1492 Columbus reached the West Indies.
1497 The English explorer John Cabot reached Newfoundland, off North America.
1498 Da Gama reached India by sea.
1519-21 Magellan sailed into the Pacific.

73

In 1492 Christopher Columbus sailed from Spain across the Atlantic to the West Indies and found a "New World" that nobody in Europe knew about. But people had been living in America for thousands of years before Europeans arrived.

Q Was Columbus the first European to sail to America?

A No. The Vikings had probably reached America in A.D. 985, but their voyages had been long forgotten when Columbus sailed.

Q How many ships did Columbus take with him?

A Columbus took three ships on his first voyage - the *Santa Maria* (his flagship), the *Nina* and the *Pinta*.

Columbus was a brave man. Da Gama knew that India existed, though he was not sure how to reach it. Columbus was sailing into the unknown.

The Santa Maria hit a coral reef in the West Indies, so only two ships made it back to Spain.

NORTH AMERICA

ATLANTIC OCEAN

WEST INDIES

Columbus found pearls in the West Indies. This made him believe he had reached China as Marco Polo's book had mentioned the Chinese diving for pearls.

Q Where did Columbus believe he was going?

A He thought he was going to China. When he got to the West Indies he insisted they were islands off China.

Q What did Columbus expect to find?

A He expected to find gold, pearls and spices because they were all mentioned in Marco Polo's book on China.

Q Why were Columbus's crews frightened on the voyage?

A They thought they were going too far from home and that in the Atlantic no wind ever blew in the direction of Spain, so they might never return!

Q Where does the name "America" come from?

A It comes from Amerigo Vespucci, an Italian adventurer, who claimed that he reached the mainland of America in 1497, but it is doubtful that he did so.

Q Did Columbus actually set foot in America?

A No. He first landed in the West Indies. Later, he made three more voyages to the West Indies. On his third voyage he reached Panama, in Central America, but he never landed on the mainland of North America.

Columbus believed the world was round, so you could reach the East by sailing west. His mistake was to think the world was smaller than it is. He thought the distance from Europe to Asia was 3,550 mi. In fact it is 11,766 mi.

SPAIN

Palos

AFRICA

Each day Columbus lied to his men about the distance they had traveled because they were afraid of sailing too far from Spain.

Ferdinand Magellan set out from Portugal in 1519, sailing westward (like Columbus) to try to reach the East. He sailed down the coast of South America and around into the vast ocean which he named the Pacific.

Q Why didn't Magellan tell his men where they were going?

A He thought they would be too frightened to obey him. Many sailors were afraid of sea monsters.

Q How long were Magellan's men in the Pacific without fresh food?

A They spent three months and twenty days eating biscuits full of grubs and drinking stinking water. They also ate rats to survive.

Ferdinand Magellan

Many sailors died of hunger and disease because they did not have fresh food supplies.

Q How was the passage to the Pacific discovered?

A Two of Magellan's ships were blown in a storm toward the South American coast. Just in time the crews spotted a small opening. It was the strait (passage) they were looking for. It is now called the Strait of Magellan.

Q Did Magellan actually sail around the world?

A No, he was killed in a battle with islanders in the Philippines.

Q How many men returned safely?

A Of the 260 or so crew aboard five ships who set out, only 18 men and one ship, the *Vittoria*, returned to Spain in 1522. They were the first people to sail right around the world.

Q What "strange" creatures did they see?

A In St. Julian Bay, South America, Magellan's men described seeing strange birds, seawolves with webbed paws at their sides, and camels without humps. These were probably puffins, seals and llamas.

Q Who led the second voyage around the world?

A Sir Francis Drake, who left Britain in 1577 to rob Spanish treasure ships did. Following Magellan's route around South America, he returned to England in 1580.

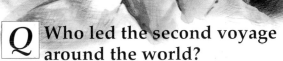

Sir Francis Drake

Who were the "conquistadors?"

Once Columbus had successfully sailed across the Atlantic, Spaniards began to explore Central America. Adventurers came to the Americas to make their fortunes. These men became known as *conquistadors* (which is Spanish for conquerors).

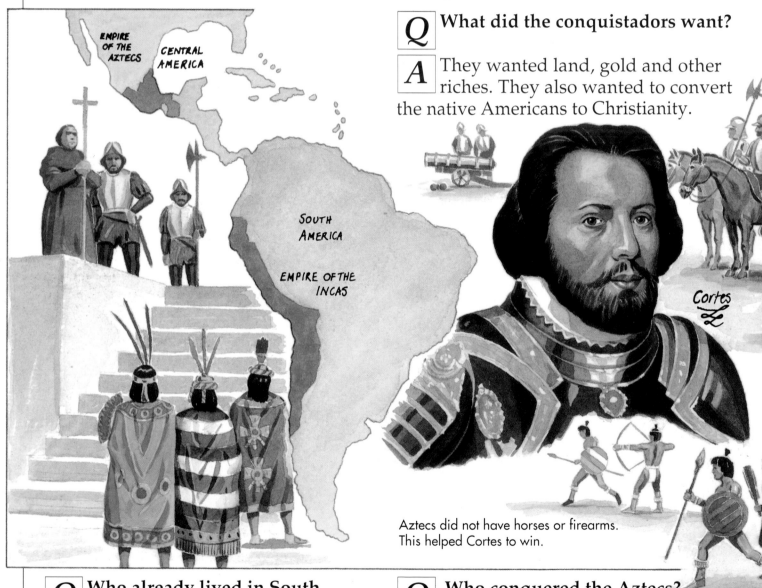

Q What did the conquistadors want?

A They wanted land, gold and other riches. They also wanted to convert the native Americans to Christianity.

Aztecs did not have horses or firearms. This helped Cortes to win.

Q Who already lived in South America?

A Many native peoples, including the Aztecs, who ruled in Mexico, and the Incas who ruled in Peru did.

Q Who conquered the Aztecs?

A The Spaniard, Hernando Cortes, landed in Mexico in 1519 with 600 soldiers and sixteen horses.

Aztecs thought one of their gods, Quetzalcoatl, had a white face and black beard - like Cortes. They believed he wore a feathered headdress, and Cortes wore a feather in his helmet.

Spaniards took cows, horses and pigs to South America.

Q How did Cortes win with so few men?

A The Aztec emperor, Montezuma, thought that Cortes might be a god and so did not fight. Later, other tribes who did not like the Aztecs helped Cortes.

Thousands of Aztecs died of European diseases that the Spanish brought with them, such as smallpox, measles and colds.

Q What happened to the Incas?

A Another Spaniard, Francisco Pizarro, defeated the Incas in 1531-33 with a small army. He captured their king, said he would release him in return for a roomful of gold, then murdered the king anyway

Pizarro

Red Pepper

Cacao Bean

Tomato

Potato

Turkey

When Drake returned to England in 1586, he brought news of tobacco, the Spanish name for a herb the Indians

Q What happened to the Aztecs?

A The Spaniards made the Aztecs slaves. They forced them to work hard in mines and on the land. Many died and within a few years the Aztec culture was destroyed.

Q What new items came to Europe from the New World?

A Tomatoes, chocolate (from the cacao bean) and red peppers came from America, as well as tobacco, potatoes and turkeys.

Who explored Africa?

Africa is a huge continent that was first explored by Europeans in the nineteenth century. Its deserts, rivers, plains and jungles were uncharted, making journeys difficult and dangerous.

Q Why was Africa so dangerous for explorers?

A Africa was such a wild place that it took very determined explorers to brave the hazards. They had to put up with disease, fierce animals, rugged surroundings and often hostile people.

Livingstone was once attacked by a lion, he survived but was badly injured.

Q Who was the greatest explorer in Africa?

A The British explorer and missionary (spreader of Christianity) David Livingstone traveled nearly 31,070 mi. through Africa from 1841 until his death in 1873. He was missing in 1866 and was not found again until 1871. He was found by the American explorer Henry Morton Stanley who used the famous greeting: "Doctor Livingstone, I presume?"

Q Who found the source of the River Nile?

A The River Nile is the longest river in the world. It flows for 4,132 mi. through North Africa to the Mediterranean Sea. John Hanning Speke, a British explorer, discovered in 1862 that the Nile flowed out of Lake Victoria.

The highest African mountain is Kilimanjaro (19,341 ft.) in Tanzania. A German, Hans Meyer, first reached the highest peak in 1889

Q Who was the most famous woman explorer of Africa?

A In the 1890s a British woman, Mary Kingsley, explored West Africa and discovered many unknown species of birds and animals. She also fought for justice and medical care for the African people.

Q Who explored the Sahara Desert?

A The Sahara is the largest desert in the world with an area of 3.5 million sq. mi. One-third of it is sand and the rest rocky wasteland. In the 1820s the Scottish explorers Hugh Clapperton and Walter Oudney, and English soldier Dixon Denham crossed the Sahara and made friends with Arab leaders.

Q What other great discoveries were made in Africa?

A The German explorer Heinrich Barth discovered the source of the Niger River in the 1850s and also discovered a new route across the Sahara Desert.

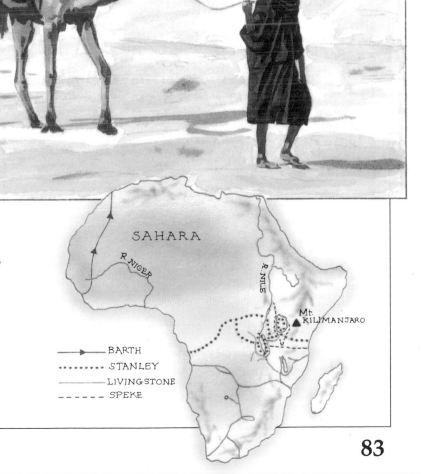

SAHARA

R. NIGER

R. NILE

Mt. KILIMANJARO

→ BARTH
······· STANLEY
——— LIVINGSTONE
– – – – SPEKE

In the second century BC, a Greek man called Antipater of Sidon decided to write about seven of the most marvellous structures that existed at the time. These became known as the Seven Wonders of the Ancient World.

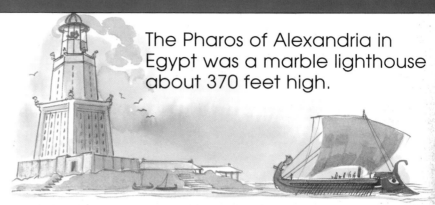

The Pharos of Alexandria in Egypt was a marble lighthouse about 370 feet high.

The pyramids of Giza in Egypt were the tombs of Ancient Egyptian kings and queens. They were buried with all the things they thought they might need in their next life, such as food, furniture, and jewels.

The statue of Zeus, King of the Greek gods, was carved from ivory and marble. It was 12 metres tall and built at Olympia, Greece.

The Ancient Greeks built temples to worship gods and goddesses. The Temple of Artemis, in Ephesus, Turkey, was built to worship the goddess of hunting and fertility.

King Mausolus decided to build himself the most elaborate tomb in the world at Halicarnassus, Turkey. A new word was invented to describe the tomb – mausoleum, after Mausolus.

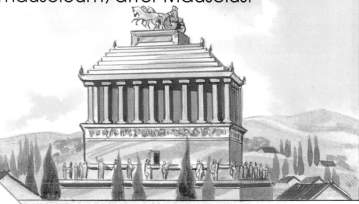

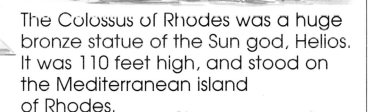

The Colossus of Rhodes was a huge bronze statue of the Sun god, Helios. It was 110 feet high, and stood on the Mediterranean island of Rhodes.

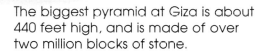

The biggest pyramid at Giza is about 440 feet high, and is made of over two million blocks of stone.

King Nebuchadnezzar built the beautiful Hanging Gardens of Babylon in Mesopotamia for his wife. Stone terraces were shaped like pyramids and filled with colorful plants.

91

Building Wonders

Amazing buildings are found all over the world. There are wonderful castles and palaces, strange houses, and very unusual stores!

In Houston, Texas, a store has been designed to look as though it is falling down!

Neuschwanstein Castle

In Germany in 1869, King Ludwig of Bavaria began building himself a fairytale castle with lots of towers and turrets.

Imagine a huge building made completely of glass. Crystal Palace was built in London, England, in 1851. Its great iron frame contained 300,000 pieces of glass.

In Beijing, China, the Emperor lived in his own private city, with palaces, lakes and gardens. Ordinary people were not allowed in, so it was called the Forbidden City.

The Biosphere, in the Arizona desert, was like a huge greenhouse, containing different habitats, each with plants and animals.

The Palace of Versailles in France is 600 yards long and is the biggest palace in the world. It was built for King Louis XIV in 1682.

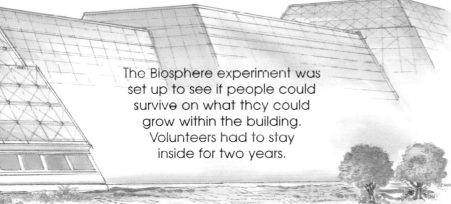

The Biosphere experiment was set up to see if people could survive on what they could grow within the building. Volunteers had to stay inside for two years.

One of the strangest houses in the world is in San José, California. Its owner, Sarah Winchester, was afraid of ghosts and believed that they would harm her unless she kept doing building work on the house. Work went on for 38 years!

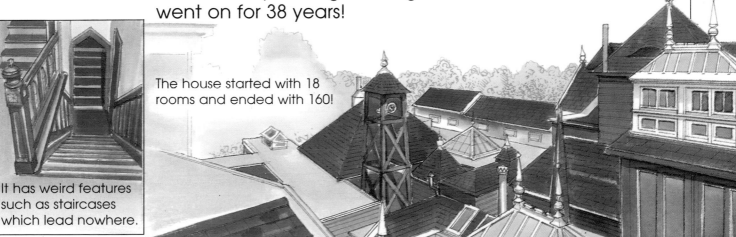

The house started with 18 rooms and ended with 160!

It has weird features such as staircases which lead nowhere.

Mountains are made when rocks under the Earth's surface move. Sometimes molten rock rises up inside the Earth and pushes the land into a dome-shape.

From the rocky desert of Monument Valley in Utah, strange towering pieces of rock rise to 1,000 feet. Water, wind, and temperature changes have worn away the surrounding rock to make shapes that look like ruined castles or crumbling skyscrapers.

Some mountains are volcanoes. A volcano is a hole in the Earth's surface. Hot molten rock (lava) inside the Earth shoots out of the hole when the volcano erupts.

The largest active volcano is Mauna Loa, in Hawaii. An active volcano is one that still erupts. Mauna Loa last erupted in 1984.

Ayers Rock in Australia is the biggest rock in the world. It is 1½ miles long and over 1,100 feet high.

One of the biggest and most terrifying volcanic eruptions was when Krakatoa in Indonesia exploded in 1883. Rock shot 15 miles into the air, and dust fell over 3,000 miles away.

Krakatoa

When Mount Vesuvius in Italy erupted in AD 79, the Roman town of Pompeii was completely buried by volcanic ash. When archaeologists dug out the town centuries later they found that the buildings and beautiful mosaics had been preserved by the lava.

The highest mountain in the world is Mount Everest, in the Himalayan mountains. It is 29,028 feet high. The first people to climb to the top were Edmund Hillary and Sherpa Tenzing Norgay, in 1953.

The longest range of mountains is the Andes in South America. It stretches for about 4750 miles.

Since ancient times, people have sculpted images of humans and gods. Some are carved from stone or wood, or cast from metal. Many of them are enormous.

In Ancient Britain, people carved giant figures and animals into chalky hillsides. The "Long Man" at Wilmington, East Sussex is 205 feet long – the largest hill carving in Britain.

An enormous statue of Jesus overlooks Rio de Janeiro in Brazil. The sculptor, Paul Landowski, built the 120-foot tall concrete statue in 1931.

On Easter Island in the South Pacific Ocean, hundreds of strange stone figures were discovered. Archaeologists think they were carved some time between AD 1000 and 1600.

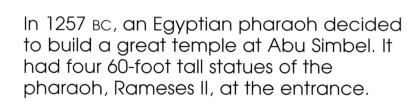

In 1257 BC, an Egyptian pharaoh decided to build a great temple at Abu Simbel. It had four 60-foot tall statues of the pharaoh, Rameses II, at the entrance.

The tallest statue in the world stands in Tokyo, Japan. This bronze statue of Buddha is 360 feet tall and weighs over 1000 tons.

One man turned a mountainside into a sculpture! Gutzon Borglum carved the heads of four American presidents on Mount Rushmore in South Dakota. It took him 14 years.

In 1501, the artist Michelangelo carved a beautiful lifelike marble statue of David, who killed the giant Goliath in the Bible story. It was sculpted out of a huge marble block which a sculptor had worked on years before, but had abandoned. Michelangelo designed his sculpture to fit into the chiselled marble block. The statue is over twice life-size.

A waterfall is formed when a river wears away the soft rock beneath a layer of hard rock to form a step.

Geysers are caused when water is heated by hot rocks under the ground. Steam pressure builds up and forces a jet of hot water out of a hole in the ground.

The highest waterfall in the world is the Angel Falls in Venezuela. It drops 3,212 feet.

One of the most famous waterfalls in the world is the Victoria Falls on the River Zambezi in Africa. Visitors have a great view of the Falls from cliffs just 250 feet away.

The Great Barrier Reef off Queensland in Australia is the biggest coral reef in the world. It is a rock-like mass built up from tiny sea creatures called corals and their skeletons.

Many sea urchins, oysters, and colorful fish live on the Reef.

On his way to California, in 1933, a sailor saw the highest ever recorded wave during a hurricane. It was just over 100 feet tall.

The tallest ever geyser shot out hot, black water and huge rocks to a height of 1,400 feet. The Waimangu Geyser in New Zealand used to erupt about every three days, but has been quiet since 1904.

Today, the tallest geyser is in Yellowstone National Park, Wyoming. Known as the Steamboat Geyser, its eruptions reach heights of up to 350 feet.

The strongest sea currents in the world reach a speed of nearly 20 miles per hour in the Nakwakto Rapids, British Columbia in Canada.

Tunnelling Wonders

Tunnels carry roads and railways beneath cities, through mountains and under the sea. Some tunnels supply water, and others take away sewage.

Tunnels may be cut out of rock by huge boring machines. Some tunnels are built in sections and then buried.

Tunnels allow canals to pass through hills. Up until the mid-1900s, canal boats were guided through tunnels by men called 'leggers'.

The Channel Tunnel is the world's longest tunnel under the sea. It travels 30 miles under the English Channel between England and France.

The Channel Tunnel was dug out by enormous machines with 100 cutters and 200 teeth. They chewed through the rock and passed it backwards to be taken away on trains.

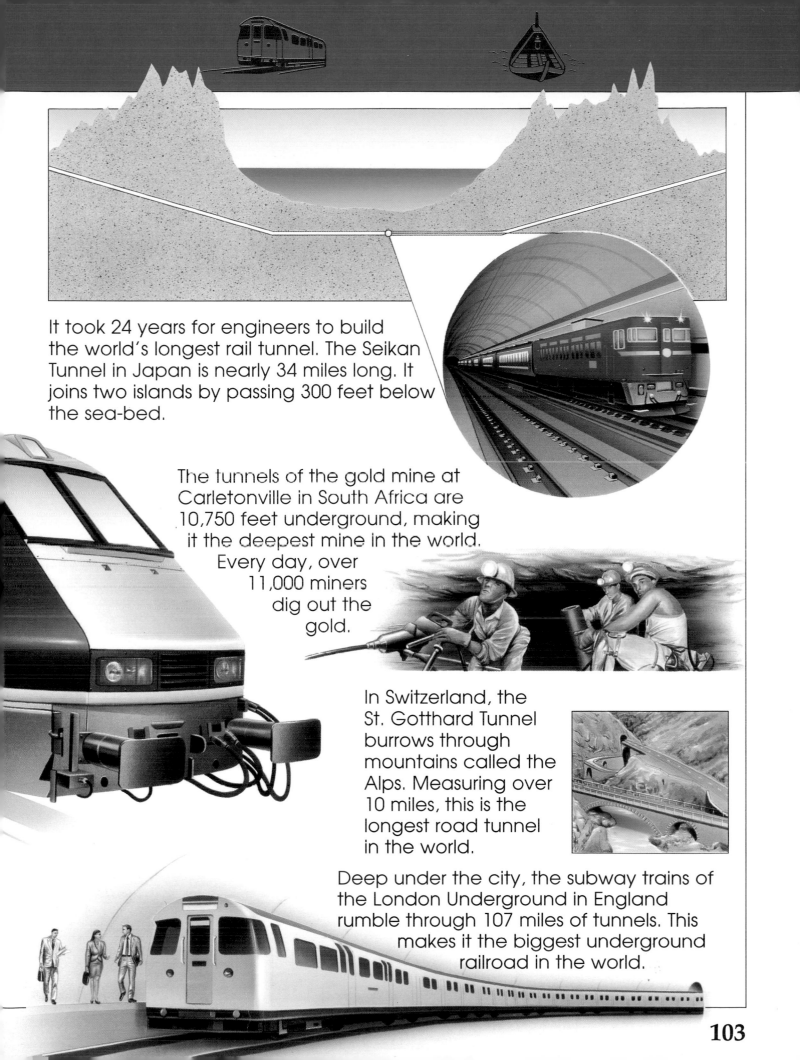

It took 24 years for engineers to build the world's longest rail tunnel. The Seikan Tunnel in Japan is nearly 34 miles long. It joins two islands by passing 300 feet below the sea-bed.

The tunnels of the gold mine at Carletonville in South Africa are 10,750 feet underground, making it the deepest mine in the world. Every day, over 11,000 miners dig out the gold.

In Switzerland, the St. Gotthard Tunnel burrows through mountains called the Alps. Measuring over 10 miles, this is the longest road tunnel in the world.

Deep under the city, the subway trains of the London Underground in England rumble through 107 miles of tunnels. This makes it the biggest underground railroad in the world.

Entertaining Wonders

Throughout history, people have created magnificent structures for entertainments.

Sydney Opera House overlooks Sydney harbor in Australia. It is shaped like a series of shells and is covered in tiles which catch the light. There are five separate halls inside.

Las Vegas, Nevada, has many buildings lit with neon lights.

The Romans built the Colosseum in Rome, Italy. It was a huge sporting arena. Up to 50,000 people would come to watch gladiators fight.

Walt Disney World in Florida, is the biggest amusement park in the world. It takes five days to look round all of it!

The longest roller coaster ride in the world is at Lightwater Valley Theme Park in Yorkshire, England. It is over 1¼ miles long.

In Ancient Greece, open-air theaters were very popular. At the Epidaurus theater, 14,000 people could watch a play. Actors on stage could be heard even if you sat right at the top.

The four-story Colosseum can still be seen in Rome. It is 160 feet high, and measures 1,600 feet round.

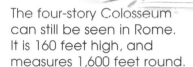

The biggest football stadium in the world is in Rio de Janeiro in Brazil. It can hold a crowd of 205,000 people.

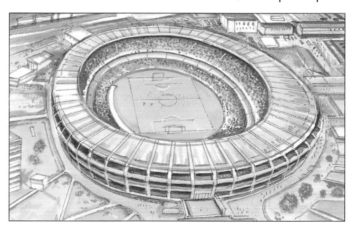

The Superdome in New Orleans, Louisiana, is the largest indoor stadium in the world. In Toronto, Canada, SkyDome Stadium, shown below, has the biggest moving roof in the world. It is rolled back in summer.

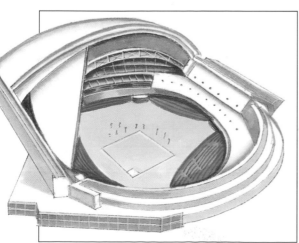

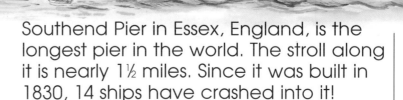

Southend Pier in Essex, England, is the longest pier in the world. The stroll along it is nearly 1½ miles. Since it was built in 1830, 14 ships have crashed into it!

Underground Wonders

Caves are formed
when rainwater
gradually wears
away rock, and
streams work their
way underground.
The streams form
tunnels which
slowly grow
into caves.

In the Cueva de Nerja, Málaga, Spain, hangs a 180-foot stalactite – the longest in the world. The tallest stalagmite in the world is in the Krásnohorská cave in Slovakia. It is 100 feet tall.

In Kentucky,
explorers have found
the biggest collection
of connected caves
in the world.
The Mammoth
Cave system covers
350 miles.

The deepest cave in the world is at Réseau Jean Bernard in France. It is nearly 5,000 feet deep.

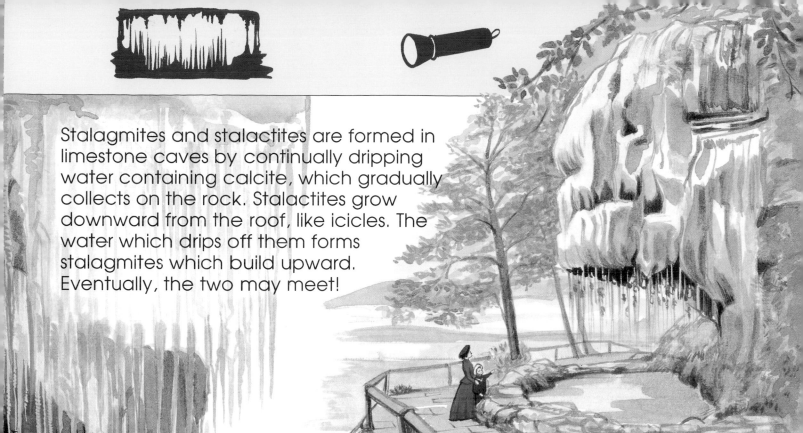

Stalagmites and stalactites are formed in limestone caves by continually dripping water containing calcite, which gradually collects on the rock. Stalactites grow downward from the roof, like icicles. The water which drips off them forms stalagmites which build upward. Eventually, the two may meet!

Since the sixteenth century, people in Knaresborough, England, have hung objects at the Dropping Well. Dripping water gradually turns the objects to stone. This happens in the same way as stalactites are formed.

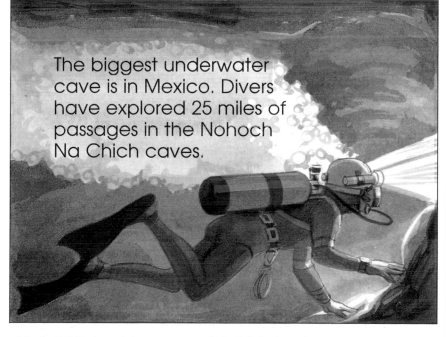

The biggest underwater cave is in Mexico. Divers have explored 25 miles of passages in the Nohoch Na Chich caves.

At 2,500 feet long and 1,000 feet wide, with a roof at least 250 feet high, the biggest cave in the world is the Sarawak Chamber, Lubang Nasib Bagus, in Sarawak, Malaysia.

Artists have created exciting works of art in many different forms, from painting and sculpture to textiles and glass.

The oldest artistic wonders date back to 30,000 BC, when Palaeolithic people created cave pictures using mineral powder.

One of the earliest ways to decorate walls was by mosaic. Using tiny pieces of glass, stone, or marble, artists put together colorful pictures like amazing jigsaw puzzles.

The first cartoon strip in the world was embroidered in wool in the eleventh century! The Bayeux Tapestry tells the story of how the French conquered England in 1066. It is 231 feet long.

A battle scene from the Bayeux Tapestry.

This mosaic of the Empress Theodora is in a church in Ravenna, Italy. It was made in the sixth century AD.

Pablo Picasso produced more works of art during his life than any other artist. When Picasso died at the age of 78 in 1973, he had created around 148,000 pieces. His cubist paintings show several views of an object at the same time.

Stained glass windows in Christian churches were used to teach people about the Bible. This window in Cologne Cathedral in Germany tells the story of Jonah and the whale.

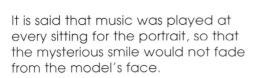

The most famous painting in the world is probably the *Mona Lisa*, which was painted by the Italian artist, Leonardo da Vinci, in about 1503.

It is said that music was played at every sitting for the portrait, so that the mysterious smile would not fade from the model's face.

Wherever the weather is very hot, dry, or cold, the landscape displays incredible features. Canyons or gorges are valleys with steep rock walls.

The biggest glacier in the world is the Lambert Glacier in Antarctica, which is over 440 miles long. The fastest-moving glacier is in Alaska, and can move about 70 feet a day.

The Vicos Gorge in Greece is 3,500 feet wide and 3,000 feet deep.

A glacier is a huge, slow-moving river of ice.

The biggest gorge in the world is the Grand Canyon, Arizona. It is between 4 and 18 miles wide and 278 miles long.

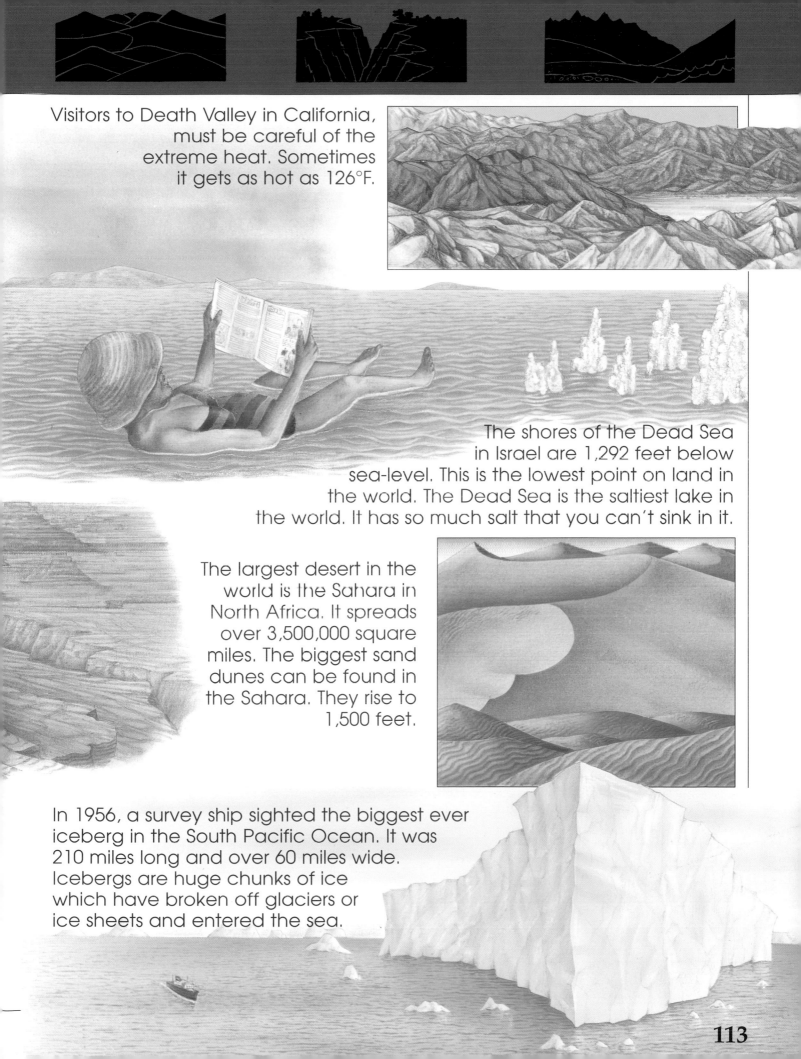

Visitors to Death Valley in California, must be careful of the extreme heat. Sometimes it gets as hot as 126°F.

The shores of the Dead Sea in Israel are 1,292 feet below sea-level. This is the lowest point on land in the world. The Dead Sea is the saltiest lake in the world. It has so much salt that you can't sink in it.

The largest desert in the world is the Sahara in North Africa. It spreads over 3,500,000 square miles. The biggest sand dunes can be found in the Sahara. They rise to 1,500 feet.

In 1956, a survey ship sighted the biggest ever iceberg in the South Pacific Ocean. It was 210 miles long and over 60 miles wide. Icebergs are huge chunks of ice which have broken off glaciers or ice sheets and entered the sea.

113

Engineering Wonders

Engineering is work that uses scientific knowledge for designing and building machines, vehicles, buildings, roads and structures such as bridges, dams and walls.

Aqueducts were first built in ancient times to carry water over a distance into cities. The Romans built the longest, which ran to the city of Carthage in Tunisia from springs 90 miles away.

Work on Britain's longest wall was started by the Romans in AD 122. Hadrian's Wall took only four years to build, and snaked nearly 74 miles across northern England.

The most concrete ever used to build a dam was poured into the huge Grand Coulee Dam in Washington State. It is 3,850 feet long and 551 feet high.

In the US, trains trundle 12 miles along the longest railway viaduct in the world. The viaduct crosses the Great Salt Lake in Utah.

Suspension bridges hang from cables between two towers. The Humber Estuary Bridge over the River Humber, England, is the longest in the world. The distance between its towers is 4,250 feet.

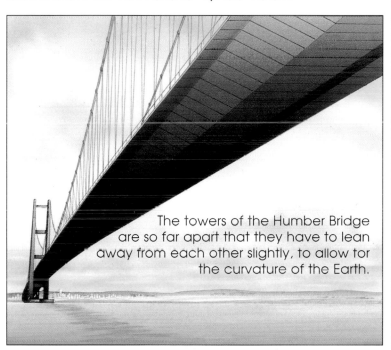

The towers of the Humber Bridge are so far apart that they have to lean away from each other slightly, to allow for the curvature of the Earth.

Sydney Harbor Bridge in Australia is the widest bridge in the world. At 150 feet wide, it carries two railway tracks, an eight-lane highway, a cycle path, and a footpath.

The longest wall in the world can be seen from Space! The Great Wall of China stretches 2,165 miles along a mountain range. The wall was built to keep invaders out of China. Builders worked for over a hundred years to finish it in about 210 BC.

Phenomenal Wonders

A phenomenon is any remarkable occurrence. Natural phenomena are those which occur in nature.

A comet is a rocky object which travels around the Sun and can periodically be seen from Earth. Halley's Comet was first recorded in 240 BC.

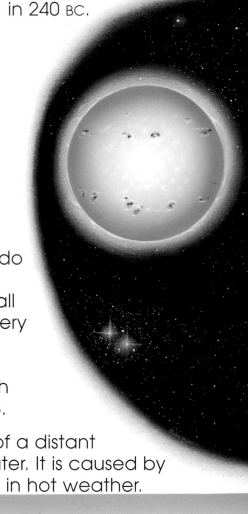

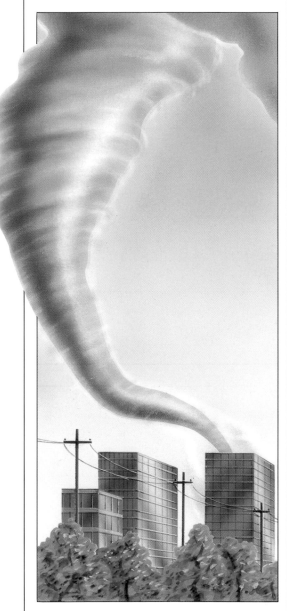

A waterspout is a tornado which has formed over water, and created a tall spinning column of watery mist. The highest waterspout reached 4,600 feet off New South Wales, Australia, in 1898.

A mirage is the illusion of a distant object or a sheet of water. It is caused by atmospheric conditions in hot weather.

A tornado looks like a tube reaching out of a cloud. Its spiralling winds may reach over 300 miles per hour.

A solar eclipse is when the Moon passes between the Sun and the Earth. The longest solar eclipse in recent times was in 1715, and lasted four minutes.

Meteorites are broken bits of comets or asteroids which fall to Earth. The biggest one ever found was 9 feet long and weighed 60 tons. It was found in Namibia, Africa, in 1920.

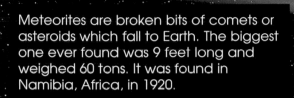

Hailstones form when water droplets in storm clouds freeze and fall to Earth. The heaviest hailstones fell in Bangladesh in 1986. They weighed 2.2 pounds and killed 92 people.

The northern lights, or aurora borealis, are different coloured bands of light that move across the sky in the polar region. They are caused by particles from the Sun reaching the Earth's magnetic field.

St. Elmo's fire is a luminous area which may appear around objects such as church spires, ships' masts, or aircraft wings. It is caused by electricity in the atmosphere.

INDEX

Created by Zigzag Publishing, a division of Quadrillion Publishing Ltd, Godalming Business Centre, Godalming, Surrey GU7 1XW, England.

This edition contains material previously published under the titles Zigzag Factfinders/100 Questions & Answers - *Ancient Times, Warriors, Explorers,* and *Wonders of the World.*

Color separations: RCS, Leeds, England, and ScanTrans, Singapore
Printed by: Tien Wah Press, Singapore

Distributed in the U.S. by SMITHMARK PUBLISHERS a division of U.S. Media Holdings, Inc., 16 East 32nd Street, New York, NY 10016

Copyright © 1997 Zigzag Publishing. First published 1995
First published in 1994 by Zigzag Publishing Ltd

ISBN 0-7651-9349-3
8458